Physicians' Guide to the Diagnosis and Treatment of Depression in the Elderly

Edited by
Thomas Crook, Ph.D. and Gene D. Cohen, M.D., Ph.D.
Center for Studies of the Mental Health of the Aging
National Institute of Mental Health

Published by
Mark Powley Associates, Inc.

ISBN: 0-943378-00-1

Physicians' Guide to the Diagnosis and Treatment of Depression in the Elderly

Contributors

Nancy Andreasen, M.D., Ph.D.

Elaine M. Brody, M.S.W.

Joseph DiGiacomo, M.D.

Gary Emery, Ph.D.

Max Fink, M.D.

Lissy F. Jarvik, M.D., Ph.D.

Robert Kastenbaum, Ph.D.

M. Powell Lawton, Ph.D.

Robert Prien, Ph.D.

Carl Salzman, M.D.

Joseph Wolpe, M.D.

Thomas Crook, Ph.D.   Gene D. Cohen, M.D., Ph.D.

Dr. Crook is Head of the Drug and Alcohol Program at the Center for Studies of the Mental Health of the Aging at the National Institute of Mental Health in Rockville, Maryland and Dr. Cohen is Chief of the Center.

Preface

The purpose of this publication is to provide physicians with a concise, practical guide to the diagnosis and treatment of depression in elderly patients. Throughout the book the focus is on practice rather than theory.

The authors of the chapters are leading national and international experts in their fields. They have attempted to translate accumulated research findings and extensive clinical experience into straightforward information for physicians providing primary medical care for aged patients.

The first chapter, by Dr. Nancy Andreasen, provides guidelines for diagnosing depression in the elderly and for distinguishing between diagnostic subtypes relevant to treatment. In chapter 2 Dr. Carl Salzman discusses the many conditions in which either a physical disease or a treatment for a physical disease may give rise to depression in the elderly. Of course, depression may also result from nonsomatic factors, and in chapter 3 Dr. Powell Lawton discusses the powerful psychosocial and environmental stresses of later life that may lead to the disorder. Chapter 4, by Dr. Elaine Brody, provides an insightful discussion of issues that may guide the physician in dealing with the families of depressed elderly patients. In chapter 5 the focus of the book shifts to treatment, with a clear discussion of state-of-the-art pharmacologic treatment by Drs. Joseph DiGiacomo and Robert Prien. A second form of somatic treatment is discussed in chapter 6, where Dr. Max Fink focuses on electroconvulsive therapy. Chapters 7 and 8 provide unusual and creative guides to the application of two major forms of psychotherapy in the practice of medicine. In chapter 7 Dr. Joseph Wolpe, the foremost pioneer in behavior therapy, describes the application of his systematic desensitization procedure and other behavioral techniques in selected elderly depressed patients. Another creative psychotherapeutic technique that can be applied in medical practice is cognitive therapy, described by Dr. Gary Emery in chapter 8. Finally, in chapter 9, Dr. Robert Kastenbaum discusses the problem of suicide in elderly patients.

We thank the authors for their thoughtful and skillfully crafted papers. We also thank the Ciba Pharmaceutical Company, whose commitment to medical education made widespread distribution of this publication possible.

It is our hope that this book will provide physicians with a valuable resource for dealing with depression in elderly patients. This is a particularly important topic, because depression is not only widespread among the aged, but it is also a disorder that usually responds to appropriate intervention. Certainly, there can be few experiences in medicine more rewarding than helping to transform the later years of an individual's life from a time of incapacity, despair, and self-denigration to a time of productivity, confidence, and self-integrity.

Thomas Crook, Ph.D.
Gene D. Cohen, M.D., Ph.D.

Contents

Dr. Jarvik is Professor of Psychiatry at the University of California, Los Angeles School of Medicine and Chief of the Psychogeriatrics Unit at the Brentwood Veterans Administration Medical Center in Los Angeles. She has published and lectured extensively on the topic of depression in the elderly, and on such other topics as senile dementia, genetics and psychopharmacology. Dr. Jarvik is a past president of the American Psychological Association's Division on Adult Development and Aging, and is currently Chair-Elect of the Gerontological Society's Section on Clinical Medicine.

Introduction

Lissy F. Jarvik, M.D., Ph.D.

More than 25 million people in the United States today have
reached or passed the age of 65 years, that arbitrary point at which
the individual is considered by many to have joined the ranks of the
elderly. This figure represents one in nine Americans, and if current
trends continue, the proportion will reach one in five within the next
50 years. The significance of this demographic shift for physicians
providing primary medical care may be appreciated if one considers
that, even today, persons over the age of 65 account for more than
30% of the visits to specialists in internal medicine.

Among the large and growing elderly population, depression is
generally regarded as the most prevalent mental health disorder. In
fact, the prevalence of depression is higher among the elderly than in
any other age group, as is the risk of suicide. Approximately 10% of
elderly individuals in the general population may suffer from depression, and among elderly patients seen by physicians providing
primary medical care the rate is likely to be much higher as a result
of two factors. First, depression is closely related to medical illness
in the elderly, and second, depressed aged patients may be more
likely than young adults to seek the help of their personal physician
rather than a psychiatrist, psychologist, or other mental health
professional.

Thus, it is important for physicians to be familiar with the clinical
picture of depression in the elderly, the factors that may give rise to
the disorder, and the effective options available for treatment. It is to
these issues that the following chapters are addressed.

Dr. Andreasen is Professor of Psychiatry at the University of Iowa. She has extensive clinical teaching and research experience and is the author of nearly one hundred publications in diverse areas of psychiatry. Dr. Andreasen served as a member of the American Psychiatric Association task force that developed the current diagnostic nomenclature in psychiatry and has written and lectured extensively on issues related to the diagnosis of depression and other mental health disorders.

Chapter 1

Diagnosis of Depression in the Elderly

Nancy Andreasen, M.D., Ph.D.

In the daily practice of medicine, it is often difficult to determine if a patient is clinically depressed. On the one hand, patients may appear to suffer from depression when, in fact, their affective state simply reflects transient unhappiness associated with an unpleasant life event or the effects of another underlying medical or psychiatric condition. On the other hand, patients suffering from depression may not appear sad or despondent and may seek treatment for a seemingly unrelated physical or mental problem. In elderly patients the task of differential diagnosis is often even more difficult.

The objective of this chapter is to outline the symptomatology of depression in the elderly, identify subtypes of depression relevant to treatment, consider the issue of "masked depression" in the elderly, and provide guidelines for distinguishing between depression and other psychiatric disorders in persons of advanced age. Chapter 2 will consider medical conditions in which the disease itself or treatments for the disease may be associated with depression.

SYMPTOMATOLOGY OF DEPRESSION IN THE ELDERLY

Patients with depression suffer from "dysphoric mood"—an unpleasant, painful, emotional state characterized by feelings of sadness and, often, anxiety. In addition, a number of related symptoms are usually present. Most psychiatrists are reluctant to consider a depressive syndrome clinically significant unless a patient displays dysphoric mood and at least four of the other symptoms listed in Table 1.

TABLE 1

Core Symptoms of Depression

Dysphoric Mood
Appetite disturbance or significant weight change
Insomnia or hypersomnia
Psychomotor agitation or retardation
Decreased interest, pleasure, or sex drive
Loss of energy or fatigue
Feelings of worthlessness, self-reproach,
    or excessive guilt
Difficulty in thinking or concentrating
Recurrent thoughts of death or suicide

For a diagnosis of depression, these characteristic symptoms must occur together in a cluster that persists for at least two weeks. Patients experiencing simple unhappiness in response to life situations may have many of these symptoms, but the symptoms are either of relatively brief duration or they occur intermittently, rather than persisting together in a cluster. Often such patients recognize that their sadness is a normal reaction to a difficult situation and do not seek treatment.

SUBTYPES OF DEPRESSION RELEVANT TO TREATMENT

Although a syndrome characterized by dysphoric mood and a persistent clustering of the symptoms outlined is usually considered clinically significant, several distinctions are frequently made before deciding upon a course of treatment. The first distinction is between unipolar and bipolar depression. The term "bipolar" refers to those patients with a history of one or more episodes of manic behavior and is generally synonymous with the older term "manic depressive psychosis." Unipolar patients have no such history, and among these patients an important distinction is made between "endogenous" and "nonendogenous" depression.

Originally the term "endogenous" was used to refer to depressions that seemed to "rise from within," presumably as a result of some neurochemical change. Depressions that seemed to develop as a result of a painful life event, on the other hand, were frequently termed "reactive" depressions. In current usage, however, the term endogenous describes a particular set of symptoms that have been shown to predict favorable response to somatic therapy. As illustrated in chapter 7, some types of nonsomatic therapy may be appropriate only in nonendogenous depression. It should be noted that endogenous depression may, in fact, arise following a painful life event.

Typical "endogenous" symptoms are listed in Table 2. Several of these symptoms are "vegetative" or "somatic," supporting the concept that a neurochemical abnormality underlies endogenous depression.

TABLE 2

Symptoms of Endogenous Depression

Inability to experience pleasure (anhedonia)
Distinct quality of depressed mood
Diurnal variation
Terminal insomnia
Marked psychomotor agitation or retardation
Significant anorexia or weight loss
Excessive or inappropriate guilt

Other evidence for a neurochemical basis includes studies showing hypersecretion of cortisol in endogenous depression and failure to suppress cortisol secretion following dexamethasone administration. Based on this phenomenon, a dexamethasone suppression test is used by some psychiatrists in diagnosing endogenous depression, but the test is probably not suitable, at present, for application in general practice. Although false positive findings appear to be rare, the test identifies only about half of elderly patients who meet the clinical criteria for a diagnosis of endogenous depression.

In the diagnosis of endogenous depression, it is important to consider the symptoms listed in Table 2. The reference in the table to diurnal variation refers to a pattern of mood change in which the patient typically feels most depressed upon awakening in the morning and slightly better as the day progresses. The reference to a distinct quality of depressed mood reflects the perception by endogenous patients that they feel quite different than when they experienced a loss, such as the death of a loved one. Endogenous patients also frequently report an unreactive quality of anhedonia, so that they are no longer able to respond to things that they previously enjoyed. Patients with two or more of these characteristic endogenous features are more likely to respond well to the somatic therapies than are patients who lack them. Patients who are clinically depressed but who lack endogenous features often respond well to psychotherapy alone.

MASKED DEPRESSION

Although most depressed patients present with dysphoric mood, depression may sometimes be masked by another chief complaint. Some patients may not recognize that their main complaint is a feeling of sadness, while others may recognize the feeling but consider it inappropriate to discuss their mood with the doctor. Consequently, the clinician should be alert to the fact that a clinically significant depression may present first in the form of some other chief complaint.

Common chief complaints that mask depression in the elderly include such physical symptoms as headache, constipation, and nausea. Even after a physician has documented the presence of a full depressive syndrome, a patient may resist recognizing the condition and insist on treatment for the physical symptom. Depression may also manifest itself as a complaint about cognitive symptoms, such as memory loss, or difficulty in thinking. These symptoms are very common features of depression and are particularly common in elderly patients.

Because persistent insomnia is also a common feature of depression and a common complaint in the elderly, patients may also present with complaints of inability to sleep. Other patients in whom agitation is a prominent symptom may complain bitterly of a terrible feeling of nervousness or internal restlessness. Because depression can present in a variety of ways, it is important that the clinician be alert to its possible presence and take a detailed history, seeking to determine whether the core symptoms of depression are present in sufficient numbers and for an adequate period of time. When physicians begin to take such a careful history and attempt to elicit the core symptoms of depression, they are often astonished to discover how common depression is in elderly patients.

DISTINGUISHING DEPRESSION FROM OTHER PSYCHIATRIC CONDITIONS

Depression must be distinguished from several other psychiatric disorders in the elderly. Distinguishing depression from senile dementia and other organic mental disorders may be particularly difficult. In fact, the term "pseudodementia" is used to describe a true depressive condition in which cognitive symptoms are so prominent that the patient appears demented. There is no definitive test to distinguish senile dementia from pseudodementia, but several things will assist the clinician in differential diagnosis. A careful history may reveal past episodes of depression or a strong family history of depression, suggesting the likelihood of a depressive disorder. On the other hand, if the history indicates that the condition has been developing slowly over two or three years, that the patient has a history of hypertension and small strokes, or that there is a strong family history of dementia, the diagnosis of multi-infarct dementia or Alzheimer's disease is more likely. Other procedures of some diagnostic utility include psychological testing for organicity and a computerized axial tomography (CAT) scan to determine whether ventricular enlargement or cortical atrophy exists. None of these laboratory tests is definitive, however, and ultimately the diagnosis must be a clinical one. Clinicians often choose to err on the side of overdiagnosing depression, since a favorable response to treatment will spare the patient a tragic and incapacitating disorder, while a failure to respond will simply help to confirm the diagnosis of dementia. It is important to recognize that depression and dementia may also coexist, and in such cases successful treatment of the depression will lead to an improvement in the patient's overall clinical condition.

Patients with very severe depressive illness may become psychotic; that is, they may experience delusions or, less frequently, hallucinations. Delusions often center on somatic function or on the belief that someone is persecuting or trying to harm the patient. In such cases it may be difficult for the physician to distinguish between depression and other psychotic disorders of late life. For example, paraphrenia is a disease that usually begins after age 50; is characterized by agitation, suspiciousness, and delusional thinking; is often precipitated by visual or especially hearing impairment; and may be worsened by tricyclic antidepressants. The differential diagnosis is assisted by careful history taking and by obtaining a hearing test.

Chronic schizophrenia in an elderly patient may look like depression to a clinician unfamiliar with an individual case. Usually, however, with an adequate history the differential diagnosis is quite simple. Schizophrenia is a chronic mental disorder beginning early in life, or at least before age 40, whereas affective disorder is more episodic and may begin at any age. Although patients with depression may sometimes experience delusions or hallucinations, these typically have some relation to their depressed mood. The schizophrenic patient, on the other hand, experiences hallucinations that typically do not have an affective quality. It is worth noting that depressions in the elderly characterized by psychotic symptoms often are less responsive to treatment with tricyclic antidepressants than are other types of depression.

The possibility of an anxiety disorder must also be considered. Many patients with agitated depression complain bitterly about feelings of internal restlessness, inability to sit still, and symptoms of psychic anxiety such as fearfulness. These patients may pace, wring their hands, pick at their hair or clothing, and generally appear extremely anxious. In such patients the distinction between an affective disorder and an anxiety disorder can be very difficult. The attempt to make such a distinction is usually based on history. Anxiety disorders tend to be chronic or lifelong, while affective disorders are more episodic. When in doubt, the clinician is usually safer treating the patient for depression, since many anxiety disorders respond to antidepressant drugs, while serious depressive disorders rarely respond to minor tranquilizers.

SUMMARY

The diagnosis of depression in the elderly patient is a complex task. It is of critical importance for the physician to recognize depression, however, and to further distinguish between endogenous and non-endogenous types of the disorder. As will be illustrated in chapters 5–8, effective treatments for depression are available, and this distinction is relevant to the choice of treatment. It is also critical for the physician to recognize depression that may result from an underlying, and sometimes treatable, medical condition. It is to that task that the following chapter is addressed.

REFERENCES

1. American Psychiatric Association. *Diagnostic and statistical manual of mental disorders* (3rd ed.). Washington, D.C.: Author, 1980.

2. Busse, E.W. & Pfeiffer, E. (Eds.). *Mental illness in later life.* Washington, D.C.: American Psychiatric Association, 1973.

Dr. Salzman is Director of Psycho-pharmacology at the Massachusetts Mental Health Center and Associate Professor of Psychiatry at Harvard Medical School. He has extensive research, teaching, and clinical experience in geriatric psychiatry and is the author of many publications on the causes and treatment of depression in the elderly. Dr. Salzman has served in a number of national leadership roles in geriatric psychiatry, including consultant to the National Institute of Mental Health.

Chapter 2

Depression and Physical Disease

Carl Salzman, M.D.

It is important for physicians to recognize that depression is often
associated with physical disease in elderly patients and may arise in
four ways: (1) as a response to physical illness, (2) as part of physical
illness, (3) as a result of treatment of physical illness, and (4) masked
by vague physical symptoms that mimic physical illness.

DEPRESSION AS A REACTION TO PHYSICAL ILLNESS IN THE ELDERLY

Physical illness is a frequent and recognizable precipitant of depression in the elderly. Among the physical illnesses that may result in
depression are myocardial infarction, cancer, arthritis, diabetes,
glaucoma, and stroke. Factors that determine the severity of depression following physical illness include (1) the organ system involved
and its role in the maintenance of life, (2) the degree of importance
to the elderly patient of the lost functioning, and (3) the ability to
maintain a positive body image while acknowledging the loss of
parts or of function.

Cardiovascular disease, which is common in old age, regularly
produces severe depressive illness; the more severe the disease, the

more profound the depression. Depression following myocardial infarction often appears early and includes a gloomy preoccupation with the future, which patients tend not to discuss with their physicians. As the depression progresses, fatigue and exhaustion set in (sometimes falsely attributed to a failing heart by the sick patient), often followed by irritability, anxiety, dependency, and boredom. Increased dependency fosters further regression, greater helplessness, and social isolation, all of which contribute to the maintenance of depression.

The inevitable result of a diagnosis of cancer is depression. The reaction to cancer results not only from the likely prospect of decreased longevity, but also from the loss of certain affected body parts through surgical treatment. Loss of function of the organs of sexual identity, or those involved with excretion, for example, may revive psychologic conflicts regarding these bodily functions. Severe depression is often seen in the cancer patient, as well as in other patients, after surgical operations on the bowel with establishment of a colostomy. The depression sometimes includes feelings of hatred and condemnation, worthlessness, weakness, mutilation, and body disfigurement.

Patients of all ages with chronic disease may become depressed about their illness. Loss of function with diseases such as stroke, arthritis, diabetes, and glaucoma may lead to a state of emotional hopelessness and depression. As in cancer patients, the intensity of the reaction to the loss of function partly depends upon the representation it has in the body image.

DEPRESSION ACCOMPANYING PHYSICAL ILLNESS IN THE ELDERLY

Depression may be part of the clinical syndrome of a number of physical diseases prevalent in the elderly, including Parkinson's disease, brain tumor, hyperthyroidism, hyperparathyroidism, pernicious anemia, carcinoma of the pancreas, uremia, and influenza.

Parkinson's Disease

Depressive affect is a common part of the clinical syndrome in Parkinson's disease. Estimates of depression ranging from 40–90% have been cited, with a higher prevalence among women. There is no relationship between the severity of the motor disturbance and the prevalence and severity of the depression. There is also no correlation between the duration of the parkinsonian symptoms and the presence or absence of depression. The depressive symptoms of Parkinson's disease include early-morning awakening, ideas of guilt and worthlessness, hopelessness, suicidal ideation, and depressed mood. The lassitude, weakness, and slowness produced by Parkinson's disease may also resemble the physical symptoms of retarded depression. Masklike faces may occasionally be mistaken for depression, and decreased speech for poverty of thought or for negativism.

Brain Tumors

Brain tumors are among the most likely neurologic diseases to present as depression. They may be metastases from the primary sites of other tumors that are common in the elderly. Symptoms of depression that might not necessarily be typical of a primary neoplasm can sometimes be attributed to the brain metastasis. Other central nervous system tumors are also associated with depression. The rise of intracranial pressure with the growth of a tumor may produce general changes in psychologic functioning that can resemble depression. These may include inattention, indifference, withdrawal, depressed or labile mood, and drowsiness.

Apathetic Thyrotoxicosis

Hyperthyroidism is more common than hypothroidism in the elderly and is more frequently seen in females than in males. One form of hyperthyroid disease that may occur in the elderly and present a particularly confusing diagnostic problem is called apathetic thyrotoxicosis. In this form of the disease, the older patient may be disinterested, quiet, and almost resigned to death. It is characterized by an appearance suggestive of senility and the presence of a small thyroid gland, and it is without the usual symptoms of thyrotoxicosis — exophthalmos, tachycardia, and smooth skin. The diagnostic criteria for apathetic thyrotoxicosis in the elderly are (1) an apathetic appearance, (2) a small goiter, (3) depression, lethargy, or apathy, (4) absence of ocular manifestations, (5) substantial muscular wasting, (6) excessive weight loss, and (7) cardiovascular dysfunction with atrial fibrillation.

Hyperparathyroidism

Hyperparathyroidism in the older patient may also present with depression as part of the clinical syndrome. Although usually considered to be a disease more common in early middle life, one quarter of the patients with this diagnosis are past 60 years of age. The depression of hyperparathyroidism is often characterized by a lack of initiative or spontaneous activity, suicidal preoccupation, fatigue, memory impairment, and irascibility. The symptoms may also include agitation, anxiety, constipation, and insomnia.

Pernicious Anemia

The highest incidence of pernicious anemia in the population is among individuals between 60 and 70 years of age. The disease is invariably associated with dementia or a fluctuating confusional state and is more likely to be misdiagnosed as presenile or senile dementia than as depression.

Pancreatic Carcinoma

Carcinoma of the pancreas is a tumor that appears most frequently in persons between the ages of 50 and 70 years. This form of cancer, in contrast to all other types of abdominal neoplasia, is most regularly associated with depressive symptoms. Patients often describe themselves as "depressed," "low down," and "down in the dumps." There is generally no loss of initiative, ambition, or perseverance, and feelings of guilt and worthlessness are uncommon. Symptoms may include anorexia, weight loss, and pain in the back of the abdomen. Patients are usually able to differentiate the symptoms from fatigue and physical illness. Other features that may distinguish the depression of pancreatic cancer from an endogenous depression include the absence, in most cases, of symptoms such as delusions, agitation, paranoia, memory loss, and suicidal thoughts. Nevertheless, inexplicable feelings of doom, hopelessness, and despair are sometimes the first symptoms of the disease, appearing weeks or months before the onset of physical symptoms. Irritability occurs in a high number of patients who have cancer of the pancreas. In this regard, the psychiatric symptomatology resembles that associated with cancer of the stomach, although in that condition symptoms generally do not include the feelings of doom that accompany pancreatic cancer.

Uremia

Urinary-tract disease with decreased renal function and elevation of the blood urea nitrogen level is common in the elderly. Depressive mood changes, apathy, and suicidal ruminations may be emotional manifestations of uremia. The depression of uremia, or the reactive depression that accompanies chronic renal disease, is frequently associated with a delirium of varying proportions. In the early stages, mood alteration may precede the delirium. Altered electrolyte balance secondary to impaired renal function may also produce depression. Severe depressions have been noted with sodium, potassium, and magnesium depletion. As maintenance hemodialysis and renal transplantation become increasingly used in the management of chronic renal disease in the elderly, mood alterations with depression are likely to become more frequent.

Viral Infection

Viral infection, particularly influenza, may be accompanied by a sudden and dramatic decline in mood. Elderly patients who are typically alert and competent may be rapidly plunged into a state of listlessness, hopelessness, apathy, and depression. They may appear to "suddenly age." At times there is a rapid decrease in memory and attention that may be mistaken for dementia. When the depression is adequately treated and normal mood is restored, cognitive functions return to their pre-influenza state.

DEPRESSION CAUSED BY DRUGS USED TO TREAT PHYSICAL ILLNESS IN THE ELDERLY

Among the drugs that may cause depression in the elderly are digitalis, reserpine, alpha methyldopa, propanolol, guanethidine, clonidine, hydralazine, diuretics, L-dopa, bromocriptine, corticosteroids, cytostatic and immunosupressive drugs, and indomethacin.

Antihypertensive Agents

Of all drugs taken by the elderly, antihypertensive agents are the most likely to induce true depression of mood. Between 50% and 70% of patients treated with antihypertensives manifest depression characterized by sadness, weakness, apathy, agitation, and insomnia. Older patients are particularly likely to experience such depression, and those with a history of previous depressive episodes are the most susceptible of all patients.

Reserpine is the antihypertensive agent most likely to produce depression. The symptoms of reserpine depression may include decreased energy, depressed mood, apathy, anhedonia, insomnia, impaired concentration, and suicidal tendencies. The characteristic features of this depressive syndrome that may help to distinguish it from true endogenous depression are the presence of anxiety, lack of guilt, and lack of self-depreciation.

Methyldopa also has depressive side effects, particularly in the elderly. The symptoms of methyldopa-induced depression include fatigue and weakness. In patients with preexisting depression, methyldopa (like reserpine) may induce a severe aggravation of symptoms.

A number of other drugs used to treat hypertension may also cause depression. For example, lassitude, fatigue, and decreased exercise tolerance may follow the use of beta-adrenergic blockers like propranolol and may be difficult to distinguish from the symptoms of true depression. Guanethidine, hydralazine, and clonidine may also produce symptoms like those of depression, including sedation, fatigue, anorexia, and constipation. Diuretics also may give rise to these symptoms as a consequence of potassium depletion.

Digitalis

Digitalis intoxication is often represented by the triad of nausea, vomiting, and mental confusion. Depression is sometimes secondary to digitalis intoxication, although less frequently than is delirium. Symptoms of depression may include apathy, weakness, and weight loss in addition to dysphoric mood.

Antiparkinson Drugs

The elderly (particularly those over 70 years of age) are predisposed to the psychiatric reactions that may accompany the treatment of parkinsonism with L-dopa. Although delirium and psychosis are more common side effects of L-dopa than is depression, 20% of patients treated with the drug complain of some symptom of depression, such as sleep disturbance, and overt depression develops in about 10% of patients. Other symptoms of depression include tearfulness, anorexia, hopelessness, apathy, and constipation. Suicidal behavior in the elderly patient generally occurs only where there is a history of prior depressions. Depression also has been attributed to the older patient's realization that L-dopa therapy will not produce a miracle cure. Bromocriptine and carbidopa, also used to treat parkinsonism, have also been implicated in causing depression.

Corticosteroids

Cortisone and related compounds are used in the elderly, not so much to replace missing adrenal secretions, but to treat other common medical disorders, such as arthritis. Exogenous cortisol can produce euphoria, lability, irritability, or paranoia. Depressive symptoms, although less common, can also occur in association with the administration of corticosteroid preparations.

Nonsteroidal Antiinflammatory Agents

Nonsteroidal antiinflammatory agents that are commonly given to elderly patients with arthritis may produce depressive symptomatology that may range from a subtle lowering of mood and reduction in enthusiasm to a frank clinical depression. Indomethacin is more likely to cause depression than are the other drugs of this class.

Anticancer Drugs

Cytostatic and immunosuppressive drugs are used as part of the treatment of cancer. All of these drugs produce toxic side effects, chiefly nausea and vomiting. Behavioral toxicity, including depression, is sometimes seen as well. Since the elderly often receive chemotherapy for cancer, such side effects must be kept in mind.

Symptoms of chemotherapeutic toxicity may include somnolence, apathy, lethargy, irritability, and weakness. Depressed mood has been noted and may be part of a more generalized neurotoxicity, particularly observed after administration of vincristine, vinblastine, 5-fluorouracil, or L-asparaginase.

PHYSICAL SYMPTOMS THAT MAY MASK DEPRESSION IN THE ELDERLY

Although medical illness, as well as drugs used to treat medical illness, may produce depression or depressive symptomatology, the opposite is also true. That is, depression may present with a variety of physical symptoms or may present as an aggravation of a pre-existing physical illness such as stroke, respiratory disease, or cardio-vascular dysfunction. Such patients may appear depressed, but vigorously deny it. Depression may be disguised so that depressed mood is not openly felt, but physical suffering is experienced instead. In severe instances, somatic preoccupation may become hypochon-driacal. Such patients seem to have a never-ending series of physical complaints and are rarely relieved to learn of their good health. This somatization and hypochondriasis may provide the diagnostician with the only clues to depression.

A variety of physical symptoms may be clues to depression in the elderly. Gastrointestinal symptoms are the most common. Patients may be preoccupied with constipation, flatulence, and abdominal pains. They may also complain of symptoms such as bad taste, burning tongue, toothaches, and vague oral discomfort, often attri-butable to ill-fitting dentures. Symptoms referable to the genito-urinary tract, such as burning urination and pains in the lower abdomen, are also frequent clues to depression. Pain, lassitude, easy fatigability, loss of strength, headaches, backaches, stiff joints, and "ache all over feelings" are more vague symptoms that may also be somatic expressions of depression. It is often unclear whether such experiences represent real physical problems, exaggerated responses to minor physical distress, or emotional problems with no physical basis.

In summary, then, it is important for the physician providing primary medical care to recognize that an intimate association exists between physical disease and depression in the elderly. It is critical that a thorough physical examination, medical history, and drug history be obtained and that physical causes of depression be con-sidered before treatment is undertaken. Of course, it is also impor-tant that the physician consider nonsomatic factors that may be related to depression in the elderly patient. It is to that topic that the following chapter is addressed.

REFERENCES

1. Salzman, C., & Shader, R.I. Depression in the elderly I. The relationship between depression, psychologic defense mechanisms and physical illness. *Journal of the American Geriatrics Society,* 1978, *36,* 253-260.

2. Salzman, C., & Shader, R.I. Depression in the elderly II. Possible drug etiologies; differential diagnostic criteria. *Journal of the American Geriatrics Society,* 1978, *36,* 303-308.

3. Verwoerdt, A. Emotional responses to physical illness. In C. Eisdorfer & W.E. Fann (Eds.), *Psychopharmacology and aging.* New York: Plenum Press, 1973, pp. 169-181.

Dr. Lawton is Director of Behavioral Research at the Philadelphia Geriatric Center and Adjunct Professor of Human Development at Pennsylvania State University. He is a leading researcher and pioneer in the environmental psychology of later life, as well as in other areas of psychology and gerontology. Dr. Lawton has filled many important national leadership roles, including the presidency of the American Psychological Association's Division on Adult Development and Aging.

Chapter 3

Psychosocial and Environmental Aspects of Depression

M. Powell Lawton, Ph.D.

Whereas the previous chapter dealt with medical and physical conditions associated with depression, this chapter will consider the major psychosocial and environmental factors associated with depression among older people. While treatment is discussed in greater depth in chapters 5–8, this chapter will provide suggestions as to how the physician might help elderly patients weather depression associated with some of these specific factors.

In a general introduction to this topic, a first question might naturally be, "How can the physician determine if a patient is depressed because of a psychosocial or environmental factor?" Fortunately, giving adequate assistance to depressed patients does not depend on having an absolute answer to this question. The important fact to bear in mind is that when a patient is depressed, *any* stress is likely to make life more difficult. If particular stresses are the cause of depression, helping the patient deal with them will be therapeutic. If the depression is caused by other factors, the assistance will nevertheless bolster the patient's remaining strengths and lighten the overall burden.

A second important point to bear in mind is that potentially stressful events and situations occur in the lives of all people, but individuals react in quite different ways to the same event or situation. Most people deal with potentially stressful events in reasonably realistic ways. Thus, we cannot assume that an event that appears stressful or an environment that appears negative is necessarily experienced as a major strain by any given individual. Even among persons who are depressed, some will find particular situations disturbing whereas others will not. It is more important for the physician to understand how a particular elderly patient perceives and evaluates life events than it is for him to know that "on the average," a particular event like loss of spouse or residential relocation is stressful.

SOME COMMON FORMS OF PSYCHOSOCIAL STRESS

It is sometimes helpful to differentiate events with a definable beginning, short duration, and end from states in which complex sequences of events occur over a long period of time.

Events as Precipitants of Depression

Pastalan has written of the "loss continuum," by which he means the succession of losses that become more frequent with age. Some of these losses are events, such as children leaving home, retirement, loss by death of spouse or others, moving from a long-term residence, or institutionalization. There is some evidence that change in and of itself may be stressful, even if the change is favorable by usual social standards. Certainly it is not difficult to find individuals for whom normally happy events such as a birthday celebration, remarriage, or moving to better housing have resulted in notable subjective stress or even depression.

We have a general idea of the relative magnitude of stress associated with most such events, whether they are losses or mere changes, but one must recognize that such judgments are statistical rather than clinical. The clinician must determine the meaning of a particular event for each individual in order to know whether it is stressful or even salient.

Bereavement, especially the loss of a spouse, is of course the major stressful event experienced by most elderly individuals. A great deal has been written about bereavement and the subject is treated again in this publication in chapter 9. Except in unusual cases, bereavement is followed by some depressive affect, often together with symptoms such as sleeplessness, loss of appetite, obsessive thoughts, guilt about the departed, or even disorientation. Depending on the strength of the person and the perceived magnitude of the loss, mild depression and other disturbances may last for several months, while continued awareness of the loss, longing, and periodic symptoms may persist for a year. All these reactions are within the range of statistical normality. What is not normal must be judged primarily by the symptoms and intensity of the depression and its persistence beyond a period of several months. Obviously, if the depression is so severe that the patient becomes delusional or self-destructive, immediate treatment intervention is necessary.

It should also be mentioned that, on the whole, research shows a notable tendency for people to reconstitute themselves following the normal grieving period, although there are clear problems associated with widowed status in our society. These problems will be discussed in the section on "states."

Retirement is viewed by many people as an end to their productive life and, therefore, a blow to their self-esteem. It is interesting that just as many view retirement as a liberation from externally imposed demands. Women who have worked experience retirement as a loss to about the same extent as do men. Retirement is also associated with longer term states, such as lowered income, lower social status, or an enforced sharing of the home territory formerly occupied during the workday solely by a nonworking spouse. The immediate postretirement period causes most people to go through a phase of establishing a new routine and new social relationships. They are usually glad to talk with the physician about their view of retirement.

"Child launching"—the departure of children from the home to lead their own independent lives—has frequently been argued to cause depression in older parents. In general—again speaking statistically—this does not seem to be borne out by research. Most children depart with normal acceptance by the parent. Some minority experience a major loss, but an equal number experience relief that another responsibility has been lifted.

Health decline, perhaps the most potent trigger for depression, is not in itself a psychosocial event. Its consequences for self-esteem are, however, immense. If one's sense of self-worth has been contingent on performing active tasks successfully, a decline or loss of physical abilities may result in depression that persists well beyond the acute phase of a medical illness.

Sustained States as Precipitants of Depression

A variety of sustained, subacute stresses contribute at least as strongly to depression as do discrete events. Many of the statuses into which older people fall are associated with continuous or repeated deprivation. For example, widowhood entails far more than the loss of a spouse. Many daily activities and social occasions are made for couples. Although there may be no wish on the part of friends to exclude the surviving member of a couple to whom they had been close, there can be awkwardness in both formal ("Bridge is for pairs, who do we pair her with?") and affective ways ("Should we mention her husband in conversation?"). There is some evidence that society provides even fewer roles for widowers than it does for widows.

The very low incomes of many older people are occasions for daily anxieties, if not actual physical deprivation. Many such people find that being cast in the role of a "poor person" who is behind in paying bills is devastating psychologically. Although most former wage earners do adjust to the loss of their earning capacity, some will feel every day the loss of self-esteem that they see as inherent in a "nonproductive" status.

Recent attention has been called to the importance of a life-style that is full of "daily hassles" in the genesis of depression and other psychological symptoms. Most such hassles are individually minor, but they add up to a state of protracted tension. Typical causes are interpersonal, especially among members of one's household. Marital discord seems to be somewhat less among older than among middle-aged couples. However, the postretirement period is frequently a time in which ordinary marital tensions are exacerbated. Especially when one family member is a caretaker and the other the recipient of care, the imbalance thus caused is apt to cause dissatisfaction on both sides. Other family members, friends, and neighbors may also be the occasion for such stresses.

ENVIRONMENTAL STRESS
AND DEPRESSION

The pervasive tendency of society to devalue old age is a constant source of stress to which most elderly persons adapt, but which may be particularly troublesome to some individuals. Subtle social behaviors such as being either excessively nice or unconsciously rejecting of an older person in casual social contact convey the message of "ageism." The media often portray the aged in unflattering ways and this message may contribute to feelings of worthlessness that are at the heart of depression. Large-scale social change is obviously necessary to "treat" this form of stress, but a particular individual may be helped by the opportunity to "sound off" about age prejudice.

In recent years one of the most potent environmental stressors for older people in urban areas has been the fear of crime. Although actual victimization is low among the aged, it is possible for the fear, whether justified or not, to restrict the individual's mobility and thus remove many of the normal sources of joy or fulfillment from life. Such activities as visiting, window shopping, or sitting in the park are often precluded, and the result may be isolation that contributes to depression. Senior centers and other organizations for older people are good sources of advice, counseling, and direct help in strengthening both physical security and the psychological attitudes of older persons toward the threat of crime.

Many older people live in deteriorating neighborhoods or housing. The lack of beauty, the scarcity of stimulation, and the departure of familiar neighbors, stores, and storekeepers may produce a feeling of isolation and panic. Economic deprivation and lack of confidence about their ability to deal with repairmen, landlords, real-estate agents, and so on may reinforce passivity in maintaining or upgrading environmental quality. Again, agencies serving the elderly can often help people with these needs.

Residential relocation, one of the most studied life changes, does seem to have negative consequences for a surprising number of elderly people, including depressively tinged "grieving for a lost home." The consequences are less negative for the physically and mentally stronger, and especially for those who make the move voluntarily and, in the process, succeed in bettering the quality of their environments. Attachment to a home of many years; the security that comes from long familiarity with a home, neighborhood, and neighbors; and anxiety regarding change combine to make older people much less likely to move than are others. For many, perhaps the majority, of these nonmovers it is probable that remaining in their homes offers a net gain in psychological security. Evidence is very clear that most older people prefer to live in their own home, independent of children, as long as their health and finances permit. If a person is depressed, it is not at all clear that establishing residence with a family member is the treatment of choice. The wishes of the particular individual must be respected no matter how bad the situation or how good the alternative may seem to an observer. For those with a wish to move, but who lack the confidence or knowledge to do so, an agency referral may be in order.

Institutionalization is a special form of residential relocation that may be highly traumatic to some people. However, research indicates that most people enter an institution only after other alternatives have been exhausted. By the time most aged individuals apply for admission to an institution, they have come to terms with the idea that they require closer supervision or closer proximity to medical care than is afforded by living in the community. It is important to recognize, however, that the state of awaiting institutionalization may be more stressful than the event of admission to an institution. Support may be particularly appropriate between the time of application and admission to an institution. To the most vulnerable, this experience may result in premature death. The event of admission and the adjustment to new physical and social surroundings is also typically acutely disrupting. Thus, support from both family and professionals is particularly important as the patient awaits admission to an institution and as he or she becomes acclimated to the new surroundings. A highly traumatic event, to the point of increasing mortality risk among the least healthy, is the involuntary transfer of residents from one home to another, as in the case of institutional closings or replacements.

WHAT THE PHYSICIAN CAN DO ABOUT STRESS RELATED TO PSYCHOSOCIAL OR ENVIRONMENTAL FACTORS

A willingness to listen is the first requirement. Listening means not only allowing the patient to talk, but attending to what is said in a manner that will allow a distinction between occasions on which some action by the physician is required and those where a mere reassuring word is enough. As indicated in the foregoing discussion, it is not safe to assume that an elderly patient will become depressed simply because he or she has experienced a negative event or occupies a devalued status. Even if a patient is clearly depressed, the problem does not necessarily relate to the negative event or devalued status. It often is reassuring to the patient for the physician to indicate an awareness that these events or situations are disturbing to everyone and may be highly stressful to some people. The best stance for the physician is to indicate a willingness to hear more, without being perceived as intruding on the patient who prefers not to talk.

When the depressed patient indicates that psychosocial or environmental sources of stress are salient, the physician will sometimes be able to give the requisite support simply by listening or by gently affirming his or her conviction that the depressive feelings have a high probability of disappearing with time (an honest and scientifically correct judgment). Beyond that, the physician may be able to enlist the help of the patient's family in addressing the problem, as discussed in the following chapter, or may refer the patient to other sources for assistance. The physician who treats many older patients will need to become something of an expert in knowing about referral sources for assistance in solving these problems. At the very least, addresses for the Social Security office, the local Area Agency on Aging (the local name will vary), the nearest community mental health center, and a senior citizen activity center should be made available. Housing assistance is harder to obtain through a central source, but the Area Agency on Aging is probably the best point of entry. Many of these agencies produce and periodically update directories of such services. A receptionist or nurse who can look up services in this way provides an invaluable service.

By projecting confidence in the depressed patient's capacities and by helping the patient learn more about available resources, the physician can often produce an immediate and significant therapeutic effect on the patient's mood. Such simple steps as having a receptionist provide the schedule of a transit system can be therapeutic if they allow patients to exert more control over their lives and counter the feelings of helplessness that are at the core of depression. Because there are so many arenas in which an older person may become dependent for either social or health-related reasons, an especially good antidote for depression is the develop-

ment of means for the aged person to feel that he or she is recipro-
cating by also helping or supporting others. Suggestions as to how
such a person may "pay back" favors by providing minor services
for a family member or friend may bolster self-esteem.

In dealing with psychosocial and environmental factors associated
with depression in the elderly, the physician will frequently find the
patient's family a major source of assistance. By working effectively
with the family, the physician may effect dramatic therapeutic results
when depression is rooted in psychosocial or environmental causes.
It is to that topic that the following chapter is addressed.

REFERENCES

1. Gurland, B. Depression and aging. In C. Eisdorfer (Ed.), *Annual review of gerontology and geriatrics* (Vol. 3). New York: Springer, in press.

2. Lawton, M. P. *Environment and aging.* Monterey, Calif.: Brooks/Cole, 1980.

Mrs. Brody is Director of the Department of Human Services and Senior Researcher at the Philadelphia Geriatric Center. She has published and lectured extensively on issues related to the families of aged persons and on such other issues as housing for the elderly and management of impaired elderly patients. Mrs. Brody is a national leader in gerontology and a past president of the 5,000 member Gerontological Society.

Chapter 4

The Physician and the Family of the Depressed Older Patient

Elaine M. Brody, M.S.W.

The primary care physician sees a larger number of depressed elderly patients and, therefore, more of their family members today than at any other time in history. Because of the loss of functional capacities that so often accompanies the chronic conditions of old age, and which may be implicated in the etiology of depression, many elderly depressed patients depend on family members for help on a day-to-day basis. They may, for example, even depend on a family member for transportation to the doctor's office or clinic. The result is that family members of older patients are generally more visible to the physician and more involved in treatment than are family members of younger adult patients. In many cases, the families of older patients present problems for the physician that are different, more complex, and more time consuming than those encountered with the families of younger patients. If these problems are not recognized and dealt with, they may constitute barriers to carrying out even the most skilled diagnosis and treatment plan for the older depressed person.

At any age, the dependency of the patient and the dependability of those meeting the patient's needs are key to the physician's relationships with family members. Though interdependence among family members exists throughout the life span, the extent to which an individual is dependent on other family members varies considerably with age. In infancy and early childhood, the individual is obviously almost totally dependent. At times of illness, therefore, prescribed medical treatment outside the hospital or clinic is generally carried out by the young parent(s), whose presence in the physician's office is expected and accepted as normal. In young adulthood and the middle years, the physician generally relates directly to the patient. In these years the family typically enters the picture only at times of acute, mostly time-limited illnesses. In the later stages of life, the balance of dependence/independence may shift again, with the family once more assuming a larger role in providing care. At this time, however, the patient's ailments and dependencies are often chronic rather than transitional or temporary, foreshadowing continuing or even increasing dependence. While there is a somewhat orderly and predictable progression in the reduction of dependence in childhood, the pattern of increased dependence in old age is highly variable. Thus, while there are normative standards by which parental behavior toward the young is evaluated, there are no such generally accepted standards to aid the physician in evaluating filial behavior toward the elderly.

The families of elderly patients differ from those of the young in a number of ways. Although younger families are not uniform in composition, those of the elderly are much more diverse. When an aged patient is married, the spouse is usually the "responsible relative," although adult children often enter the picture as well. Whereas most older men are married (77%), most older women are widowed (52%). Most of the older people who care for an impaired spouse are women. A sick older man is much more likely to be married, not only because of the discrepancy in life expectancy between men and women, but because men tend to marry women younger than themselves and therefore to have a "young" wife if they become ill. The nine million widowed older people depend primarily on their children, if they have children. Eighty percent of older people have children, and of that group 90% have grandchildren and 46% have great-grandchildren. However, there are almost five million child-less people among the elderly, who may or may not have siblings, nieces and nephews, or other relatives on whom to rely. When family members do exist, they may or may not share a household with the older patient or live close by. It is noteworthy that in the United States today, only about 16–18% of older people live with an adult child. Of course, aside from the number of family members available to the older patient, the quality of care provided will be influenced by variations in intergenerational relationships.

The nature of the relationships between older people and their adult children is one of the most misunderstood aspects of aging. The prevalent and persistent myths state that those relationships are characterized by alienation, that adult children "dump" their elderly parents in institutions, and that children generally behave less responsibly than was the case in the "good old days." Yet remarkably consistent evidence to the contrary has been developed by major streams of research: intergenerational ties remain strong; most older people live close to at least one of their adult children and see them frequently; and when older people need help, their adult children provide the vast majority of services and do so responsibly. In a major study carried out by the United States General Accounting Office, families provided aged persons with 90% of health and social services, including nursing and personal care, household mainten-ance, transportation, shopping, and many other services. Other studies have shown definitively that, in the main, nursing home placement occurs only after the family has tried all other alternatives and has exhausted itself in the process. Only about 5% of the elderly are in institutions, and families resort to such placement reluctantly. It is clear that being married and/or having children is a major fac-tor in enabling older people to avoid or delay institutionalization.

Though families of older people have continued to be steadfast and dependable, they have been doing so against greatly increased odds. At no time in history have there been so many elderly people in families, nor have they been so old. Together with other demo-graphic trends, the falling birth rate has resulted in dramatic altera-tions in the ratio of older people in need of care to those available to provide that care. That is, those who are in advanced old age today have fewer children to share the caregiving responsibilities than has been the case in the past and, since parents and their children age together, the children of the very old are most often in their late forties, fifties, sixties, and sometimes in their seventies. More than a decade ago the Social Security Pre-Retirement Survey revealed that 25% of people who were 58 and 59 years of age had at least one surviving parent. More recent data from a national survey of older Americans indicated that 40% of people between the ages of 55 and 59 have at least one living parent, as do 20% of those between the ages of 60 and 64, 10% of those between 65 and 69, and 3% of those between the ages of 70 and 79. The vast majority of these living parents are, of course, women and the percentage rises with age. Approximately two thirds of the living parents of persons 55–59 years of age are women and virtually all the living parents of persons over age 65 are women.

Physicians undoubtedly have noticed that most family members with whom they come in contact are women in the next younger generation from the elderly patient. Studies indicate that as women advance from 40 years of age to their early 60s, they are more and more likely to have a dependent parent, to spend more and more time caring for that parent, to do more difficult tasks for him or her, and to have the elderly parent in their own households. It is clear that daughters and daughters-in-law are the principal providers of care for elderly family members. These women are often under considerable stress from multiple, competing responsibilities. Not only are they experiencing age-related problems themselves, but their responsibilities may peak rather than diminish at this stage in their lives. The role of caregiver to an elderly person is often being added to their traditional roles as wives, homemakers, parents, and grandparents. Also, to a much greater extent than ever before, middle-aged women have still another role: that of paid worker in the labor force. The proportion of married women between the ages of 45 and 54 working outside the home has increased fivefold in the last 40 years, from 11% in 1940 to 56% at present. Sixty percent of all women in that age bracket now work, and it is even more surprising that 42% of women between 55 and 64 years of age are now in the work force. Although the women's movement may account for some women working, most women work because they and their families need the money.

The pressures on such women may place them at high risk for mental and physical disorders. Indeed, many middle-aged women who seek medical care for themselves may be doing so in the context of such "role strains." What affects these women inevitably affects their husbands and children, their siblings, and eventually the total family, including the older patient. A number of studies have found that care of a mentally disturbed older person often has negative effects on all family members, including young children. Negative effects may include anxiety, depression, sleeplessness, loss of time from work, or family conflict. It is not uncommon for disagreements, even bitter conflicts, to arise around questions of planning and allocating responsibilities or resources. Psychiatrist Barry Gurland speaks of the "contagion of depression," because he and his colleagues found the incidence of depression significantly higher than normal in families with a depressed older person.

The physician, then, must be sensitive to signs of depression and other symptoms of stress in family members, particularly female caregivers. The older patient's condition affects the emotional and physical lives of his or her family members and, reciprocally, their attitudes and behavior have a profound effect on the patient. It is therefore useful to understand what family members are experiencing in their own lives that may be expressed in their relationship with the physician.

It is important for physicians to recognize that they too may be caught up in family conflicts related to the care of the older patient. Physicians may face such annoying and time consuming behaviors ar over-detailed questioning about the patient's condition and prognosis, multiple phone calls and demands, repetitive inquiries by different family members requiring the doctor to go over the same ground several times, inappropriate requests for specialty consultations, and even subtle (or not so subtle) suggestions that the doctor lacks competence or could do more if he or she wished. For some families such behaviors represent the continuation or exaggeration of lifelong patterns; for others, they result from anxiety related directly to conflicts arising from the care of the aged patient.

Certainly, the physician cannot deal with all issues and solve all family problems. It saves time in the long run, however, to obtain

information at the outset about the family constellation and circumstances. Having such matters in mind can aid in formulating realistic
expectations of the family's capacities to deal with the needs of the
elderly depressed patient. The doctor's sympathetic attitude — and a
word or two conveying an understanding of the family's efforts and
difficulties — can go a long way. In addition, providing details of the
patient's condition and telling the family what to expect can obviate
much of their anxiety and questioning. Although genuine concern
and affection for the older person are generally at work, family
members may be silently asking a set of very human questions:
"How will this affect me and my family? Will I be able to help my
parent in the way the doctor recommends? Will this situation go on
and on? Will it improve? Will it get worse?" It is important that the
physician indicate to family members that depression can usually be
treated successfully and that, in the great majority of cases, symptom
remission can be expected.

At the same time that the physician seeks to address the needs of
the family and diminish distress caused by the patient's condition, it
is critical that he or she act to preserve the patient's right to manage
his or her own life. Since dependence plays a major role in the
etiology of depression, every effort must be made to exploit oppor-
tunities to foster independence. To the fullest extent possible, therefore, patients should be allowed to be autonomous, to participate in
their own treatment planning, and to make their own decisions.

The close relationship between dependence, disability, and depression also explains why any implications that power over the patient's
life has been transferred to others can be detrimental, despite the
most benevolent intentions of family and physician. The depressed
patient already feels helpless, hopeless, and has a negative self-
image, all of which are reinforced by the realities of eroding functions.
Doctor and family should collaborate to emphasize and support the
elderly individual's residual capacities, strengths, and control over
his or her own life. The opposite approach, even if meant protectively,
can diminish and infantilize the patient and intensify the depression.
In the same vein, it is worthwhile for the physician to support the
family in encouraging the elderly person to follow rehabilitative
regimens that can improve functioning and therefore independence.

Though the vast majority of adult children are well motivated and
responsible — perhaps because they want to behave responsibly and

be dependable — they may tend to "take over" too much. Acknowledging responsibility for a parent means assuming a new role. Their only prior experience in caring for a dependent person probably was in relation to their own children or, more recently, their grandchildren. In that earlier role, it was a parental prerogative to be the decision maker. Adult children may carry over into the new situation some attitudes and behaviors that were appropriate to the parental role but are not appropriate to the filial role. The doctor's own attitude toward the elderly patient can go far in communicating to the family the respect and autonomy due the patient and in restoring the sense of dignity so essential to the integrity of the human personality.

Similarly, the doctor's behavior in listening carefully to the patient's complaints and in taking them seriously can signal therapeutic optimism to the family as well as the patient. Such an approach helps to counteract the humiliation that older people feel at being "written off" or when their ills are attributed to old age rather than disease processes. Depressed older people, even more than older people in general, already feel devalued and unworthy, reflecting the attitudes of an ageist society. They and their families are often diffident about making their complaints known and many significant symptoms go unreported to any health professional. Among the reasons for such nonreporting are familiar refrains such as "I didn't want to bother the doctor" and "Nothing can be done — it's just old age."

There also is a concrete way in which the physician can be very helpful to patients and their families. In addition to mental health programs, there are many entitlements, services, and facilities for which the patient may be eligible that could ease environmental strains. These include income-maintenance programs, specialized housing, posthospital Medicare benefits (such as home health aides), dayhospitals, homemakers, home-delivered meals, and recreational services, to name just a few. At this time there are not enough services available and their availability varies regionally. Those that do exist, however, constitute a complex and confusing array. The physician cannot be expected to explore the family's needs in great depth, to have detailed knowledge about the availability and eligibility criteria of each service, to make referrals to all the various service sources, or to monitor them over time. However, the physician is in a pivotal position — as the "gatekeeper"— to introduce patients and their families to the world of services of which they are usually unaware. To do so, the doctor should know and refer his patients to the agencies in the community whose job it is to be informed about the complete range of available services and facilities, to connect older people and their families with those services, and to help to mobilize them. Examples of such organizations are Area Agencies on Aging, family counseling agencies, and hospital social service departments.

In the final analysis, although such practical help from formal sources is necessary and should be fully exploited in the interests of both patient and family, it does not fully "solve" all problems. Family members serve many functions for the depressed, dependent older person that no formal organization can replace. They provide emotional support, social contact through visiting, response in emergencies, and the knowledge that there is someone dependable on whom to rely. The physician, then, should see the family members from two perspectives. They are his or her partners in providing sustained health and mental health care to the elderly patient over long periods of time. They are also of concern as people at risk for mental or physical problems if their caring roles become unduly stressful.

REFERENCES

1. Brody, E. M. The aging of the family. *Annals of the American Academy of Political and Social Science,* 1978, *438,* 13–27.

2. Shanas, E. Older people and their families: The new pioneers. *Journal of Marriage and the Family,* 1980, *42,* 9–15.

Dr. DiGiacomo is Associate Professor of Psychiatry at the University of Pennsylvania School of Medicine and Chief of General Clinical Psychiatry at the Veterans Administration Medical Center in Philadelphia. He is trained and practices not only in psychiatry, but also in cardiology and internal medicine. Dr. DiGiacomo has published extensively in psychiatry and psychopharmacology, including a number of papers on the cardiovascular effects of psychotropic drugs.

Dr. Prien is Chief of the Affective Disorders Section in the Somatic Treatments Branch at the National Institute of Mental Health and a member of the medical faculty at Johns Hopkins University. He has published more than one hundred scientific papers in psychopharmacology and is a leading authority on the treatment of depression in both young and aged individuals. Dr. Prien has also published and lectured on the use of drugs in the treatment of organic brain syndromes, schizophrenia, and sleep disorders in the elderly.

Chapter 5

Pharmacologic Treatment of Depression in the Elderly

Joseph DiGiacomo, M.D. and Robert Prien, Ph.D.

Many depressed elderly patients respond favorably to pharmacologic treatment and, in some cases, the response is dramatic. Although the primary indication for antidepressant drug therapy is endogenous or melancholic depression, even mild depressive disorders that appear situational and have few or no vegetative symptoms may warrant a trial with drugs, particularly if other treatment approaches have proven unsuccessful.

Drugs available to treat depression in the elderly include the tricyclic antidepressants, the monoamine oxidase inhibitors (MAOIs), lithium carbonate, and several representatives of a new generation of antidepressant drugs — maprotiline, nomifensine, and trazodone. Antipsychotic drugs may also be used, alone or in combination with antidepressants, to treat certain particularly severe types of depressive disorders. Occasionally, psychostimulants, such as methylphenidate, may also be prescribed for temporary symptomatic relief of dysphoric mood.

TRICYCLIC ANTIDEPRESSANTS

The tricyclic antidepressants available in the United States are amitriptyline, amoxapine, desipramine, doxepin, imipramine, nortriptyline, protriptyline, and trimipramine. These drugs are effective in a majority of depressed patients.

Choice of Drug

There are no major differences among tricyclic drugs in overall clinical effectiveness but, as illustrated in Table 1, there are substantial differences among the tricyclics, as well as among the newer antidepressants, on such critical variables as sedation potency, potential cardiovascular toxicity, and anticholinergic effects. These factors generally dictate drug choice in elderly patients. For example, depressed patients with prominent symptoms of sleeplessness, agitation, or restlessness may benefit from drugs having high sedative potency, such as amitriptyline and trimipramine. A bedtime dose may contribute to nighttime sedation and eliminate the need for sleep-inducing medications. Less sedating drugs, such as desipramine and protriptyline, may be preferable for patients who have marked psychomotor retardation. Anticholinergic effects are of particular concern in aged patients, as discussed later in this chapter, and wherever possible, drugs with relatively weak anticholinergic effects should be chosen. Among the tricyclics, amitriptyline appears to have the most potent anticholinergic effects, and desipramine the least potent effects.

Treatment Management

Aged patients are more likely than young adults to develop adverse side effects when treated with tricyclic antidepressants. On some tricyclics, aged patients may develop a plasma concentration that is up to twice as high per unit dose as that developed by their younger counterparts. Age-related decreases in hepatic enzyme activity and glomerular filtration rate may significantly alter metabolism and elimination of tricyclics, and the sensitivity of target tissues may also be altered with age. The result is that smaller doses of tricyclics may be required to achieve a therapeutic response in aged patients than in young patients. However, as with all generalizations, there are exceptions. Some elderly patients require and will tolerate higher tricyclic doses than do younger patients. The physician must bear in mind that failure to adequately control depressive symptoms because of fear of toxicity may be more detrimental to the elderly patient than are the drug side effects themselves.

When initiating treatment with tricyclic antidepressants, it is common practice to start the medically healthy elderly patient on 25 to 50 mg per day and increase dosage by 10 to 25 mg increments on a weekly or twice weekly basis. An exception is the use of protriptyline where dosage should be started at 5 to 15 mg per day and increased in 5 mg increments if necessary. Some elderly patients respond to doses of 25 to 50 mg per day and debilitated patients may require no more than 10 mg per day. However, many depressed aged individuals require daily doses of 75 to 125 mg, and a small minority of patients benefit from doses of 200 mg per day or more. The usual dose ranges for the tricyclics and other antidepressants are provided in Table 2.

Depressed patients with mild organic brain syndrome should be started on the lowest available tricyclic dose, with weekly increases based on tolerance and response. Drugs with pronounced anticholinergic or hypotensive effects should be avoided with these patients because of possible hypersensitivity to anticholinergic toxicity and changes in blood pressure.

Before initiating treatment, it is advisable to obtain a baseline pulse, blood pressure (both reclining and 30 seconds after standing), and an electrocardiogram (EKG). Blood pressure and pulse should be monitored routinely after treatment is begun, particularly after an increase in dosage. A marked orthostatic decrease in blood pressure is an indication to reduce the dose or discontinue medication.

Following remission of symptomatology, a useful strategy is to maintain the patient on the therapeutic dose for an additional 4 to 6 weeks.[2] If symptoms do not reappear, dosage may be reduced by 10 to 25 mg every one to two weeks until about half the therapeutic dosage level is reached. This level may be maintained for an additional three to four months and then slowly reduced.

Plasma Levels

The clinical usefulness of plasma tricyclic levels in the aged is not clear, and plasma determinations are not as yet recommended for routine dosage adjustment. The effects of age on plasma levels is not well understood and further work is needed to establish the relationship between steady-state plasma levels and therapeutic effect in elderly patients. Among the problems associated with interpretation of plasma levels in the elderly is a significant age-related increase in the variability of steady-state levels for certain tricyclics. Nevertheless, plasma level determinations may be useful for selected patients who fail to show an expected therapeutic response at a given dose. For example, if a patient fails to show a therapeutic response at 125 to 150 mg per day, it may be advisable to obtain a steady-state level before proceeding to a higher dosage. Plasma levels may also be useful for avoiding overdosage in patients with a history of cardiac problems or those who are prone to development of anticholinergic toxicity. Plasma levels are also of value in assessing patient compliance in taking medication.

Side Effects

Elderly depressed patients treated with tricyclics may experience at least three troublesome side effects: orthostatic hypotension, constipation, and anticholinergic toxicity.

Hypotension

Orthostatic hypotension may pose serious problems for elderly patients, particularly patients with vascular disease or limited cardiac reserve. Problems may include dizziness, syncopal episodes with associated falls and trauma, myocardial infarction, and cerebrovascular accidents. Orthostatic hypotension may appear on the first day of treatment and may occur with each increment in dosage. Patients on tricyclic therapy should be cautioned to move slowly from the lying to the sitting and then to the standing position. Those who complain of dizziness, lightheadedness, or cold sweats after initiation of drug therapy should be suspected of having a hypotensive episode. Orthostatic hypotension is a problem with all tricyclics, but it is particularly prominent with imipramine and desipramine. If a patient is unable to tolerate the hypotensive effects of tricyclics, the physician might substitute a new generation antidepressant with minimal hypotensive effects.

Constipation

This anticholinergic-induced side effect is often treated in a perfunctory manner, despite the potential for fecal impaction in the elderly patient. The patient may feel that the discomfort of constipation is often greater than distress due to depression and may discontinue medication as a result. It is helpful to discuss the patient's bowel habits before treatment in order to determine whether a history of bowel dysfunction exists or whether constipation is a consequence of drug treatment. Tricyclic-induced constipation may be relieved by dietary supplements such as bran or by stool softeners.

Central Anticholinergic Syndrome

Elderly patients, particularly those with mild organic brain syndrome, are particularly vulnerable to the anticholinergic side effects of tricyclics. The drugs may induce central anticholinergic toxicity leading to a dose-related atropinelike psychosis. Early signs of anticholinergic toxicity include irritability and restless pacing, accompanied by a gradual decrease in mental acuity. In the later stages of a toxic reaction, there may be agitated behavior, disorientation, delusions, visual hallucinations, and possibly seizures. Arrhythmias, hyperthermia, reduced bowel motility, and urinary retention may also occur. The syndrome may be diagnosed by the intramuscular administration of 1 mg of physostigmine salicylate, which clears the psychosis in approximately 10 minutes, although the psychosis will recur in approximately 30 minutes. If central anticholinergic syndrome is diagnosed, the physician should discontinue all drugs if possible and administer sodium amobarbital to control agitation until the syndrome clears, usually in 24 to 36 hours. As noted previously, and as reflected in Table 1, the tricyclics differ from one another substantially in anticholinergic potency and, thus, their liability to induce central anticholinergic syndrome.

Other Side Effects

Other common tricyclic side effects include blurred vision, dry mouth, minor tremor, and other anticholinergic effects, as well as drowsiness, weight gain, nausea, and heartburn. The most common cardiovascular effect is tachycardia. Other side effects include convulsions, cardiac arrhythmias, and interference with cardiac conduction. Tricyclic antidepressants should be used with caution in patients with narrow angle glaucoma or prostatic hypertrophy. The drugs are contraindicated during the acute recovery period after a myocardial infarction.

Drug-Drug Interactions

Many of the drugs required by elderly depressed patients for the treatment of physical illnesses may interact with the tricyclics to produce serious medical complications. Among these drugs are certain antihypertensives, including guanethidine, methyldopa, propranolol, clonidine, and some diuretics; anti-arrhythmic agents including quinidine, disopyramide and procainamide; oral anticoagulants; thyroid hormones; L-dopa; amphetamines and other sympathomimetics; hydroxyzine; and monoamine oxidase inhibitors.[1] In view of these possible interactions, careful and comprehensive review of the patient's medical and drug history, including use of over-the-counter medications and alcohol, should be undertaken before antidepressant drug therapy is initiated. In obtaining this information, it is often helpful to have a family member present. It is also helpful in most cases to discuss the rationale for prescribing antidepressant drugs and possible drug interactions and side effects with the family members, as well as with the patient. Informed family members may be of great help in assuring that multiple medications are taken as prescribed and in reporting adverse effects resulting from drug–drug interactions.

MONOAMINE OXIDASE INHIBITORS (MAOIs)

The MAOIs are used with selected patients who fail to respond to tricyclics or who have medical contraindications to tricyclic therapy. MAOIs may also be useful with the so-called atypical depressions in which depressed mood is somewhat reactive and accompanied by hypersomnolence, lethargy, hyperphagia, and hypochondriasis. Phenelzine, a hydrazine derivative, and tranylcypromine, a non-hydrazine derivative, are the most frequently prescribed MAOIs. The chief problem with the drugs in this category is side effects, including orthostatic hypotension, tyramine-induced hypertensive crises, and adverse interactions with many frequently used medical drugs.[4] Hypertensive crises are most likely to occur with tranyl-cypromine since the drug blocks peripheral deamination of tyramine.

Before prescribing an MAOI, one should wait one week after tricyclics have been discontinued. There should be an in-depth discussion with the patient and a family member concerning dietary restrictions and potential interactions with other drugs. Only patients who can be expected to comply with the many dietary and drug restrictions should be treated with an MAOI. Caution must be exercised in prescribing the drugs to patients with poorly organized daily routines, unstable diets, and self-medication regimens. In starting treatment, blood pressure should be monitored carefully and a test dose of phenelzine (15 mg) prescribed. Dosage may be increased by 15 mg every 4 to 5 days if vital signs are stable. Elderly patients usually respond at dosage levels of 30 to 45 mg per day. A full therapeutic effect may be achieved in 3 to 4 weeks.

NEW GENERATION ANTIDEPRESSANTS

In recent years, several new types of antidepressant drugs have become available for prescription use in the United States. These drugs are reported to be as therapeutically effective as the tricyclics and to have few troublesome anticholinergic or cardiovascular side effects. Further research is necessary to develop clinical and side-effect profiles for these drugs in elderly populations. However, if the new drugs are shown to be therapeutically equivalent to the tricyclics, and the lower incidence of side effects is confirmed, they will be attractive alternatives to the tricyclics for elderly depressed patients and, quite possibly, will become the drugs of choice.

Maprotiline

Maprotiline is a member of a relatively new class of chemical compounds, the tetracyclics. The drug became available in 1981. Troublesome cardiovascular and anticholinergic effects are reported to be rare with maprotiline. The drug has a spectrum of therapeutic action and overall potency similar to that of most tricyclics. The manufacturer suggests an initial dose of 75 mg per day. Most patients respond to a dose of 150 mg daily, but daily dosage as high as 225 mg for outpatients and 300 mg for inpatients may be required in some cases.

Nomifensine

Nomifensine is a tetrahydroisoquinoline compound that is structurally distinct from the tricyclic and tetracyclic antidepressants. The drug is in the final investigational stage for marketing approval in the United States. Nomifensine is generally well tolerated in the elderly and appears to lack the cardiotoxicity associated with the tricyclics, even when taken in overdose. The drug is a stimulating rather than a sedating compound and, therefore, may be useful in psychomotor retardation but less than ideal for patients suffering from insomnia, restlessness, and agitation. The recommended dosage for young and middle-age adults ranges from 75 to 200 mg per day. The clinical effectiveness of nomifensine in elderly populations has not been extensively studied.

Trazodone

Trazodone is a triazolopyridine derivative synthesized in 1966. The drug was approved for marketing in the United States in 1982. Trazodone appears to produce few anticholinergic and cardiovascular side effects and is reported to be as effective as the standard tricyclics. The most common adverse reactions are drowsiness, lethargy, and a feeling of being drugged. Trazodone probably has the most potent sedative effect of the available antidepressants. Its value for elderly depressed patients requires careful study. The recommended dosage for adults is 150 to 400 mg per day. Dosage recommendations for elderly patients are not available.

LITHIUM CARBONATE

Lithium is indicated for the treatment of manic episodes in bipolar affective disorders, that is, disorders marked by prior episodes of both mania and depression.

Side Effects

There is no difference between young adult and elderly patients in the nature of lithium-induced side effects. However, there is a tendency for toxic effects to occur at lower plasma levels among elderly patients, and it is necessary for the physician to be familiar with the special issues that arise in treating elderly patients with lithium. This subject is treated in detail elsewhere.[3] Among the side effects that require careful monitoring in elderly patients are the following.

Toxic Confusion

An initial sign of lithium toxicity in the aged may be confusion, accompanied by neuromuscular irritability, coarse tremor, ataxia, slurred speech, and impaired consciousness. This confusional state can progress to a coma and may be accompanied by a continuing increase in blood-lithium levels after administration of the drug has been discontinued.

Thyroid Disorders

Lithium can induce thyroid pathology, and this is particularly important in the elderly since hypothyroidism can simulate symptoms of depression and dementia.

Renal Damage

Controversy exists concerning the effects of lithium on the kidney, and it is strongly advised that physicians treating elderly patients monitor such parameters of renal functions as serum creatinine and blood urea nitrogen levels before treatment and at intervals of six months or so during treatment. Other tests that may be considered in assessing renal status are creatinine clearance, urine specific gravity after a period of water deprivation, tests of urine osmolality, and 24-hour urine volume.

Interactions With Diuretics and Low-Salt Diets

Elderly patients are more likely than young adults to have hypertension and other conditions that are treated with thiazide diuretics, or that may require dietary sodium restriction. Thiazide and other proximal tubule diuretics can significantly reduce lithium clearance and may elevate plasma-lithium levels by 25% to 30%. This may result in lithium intoxication if lithium dosage is not lowered accordingly. Low-salt diets can also result in lithium retention to the point of intoxication and present much the same problem for lithium therapy as do the diuretics.

Cardiac Effects

Lithium may aggravate existing arrythmias and conduction defects. Thus, a thorough medical evaluation and EKG should be performed prior to treatment with the drug.

Treatment Management

The initial dose of lithium carbonate in elderly patients may be 300 mg per day, with gradual increases until therapeutic effects are achieved. In general, it is not wise to increase the dose by more than 300 mg per day every 3 or 4 days. Plasma-lithium levels of 0.6 to 0.7 milliequivalents per liter are often satisfactory for maintenance treatment and even for the treatment of some acute episodes. These levels are usually achieved with doses of 600 to 900 mg per day, although higher doses may be required for the more severe manic attacks.

To guard against the presence of an undetected impairment in renal function which could lead to the rapid onset of lithium toxicity, plasma levels should be obtained 2 and 4 days after the initial dose, at least twice each week during titration, and each month or two after clinical remission when dosage is stabilized.

During long-term treatment the patient's clinical and physical status, as well as plasma levels, should be continuously monitored. In addition to periodic physical examinations, monitoring should include laboratory tests of renal electrolyte and thyroid functioning, complete blood counts, and electrocardiographic assessment. Dosage reduction may be required if there is sodium loss or impaired renal function from factors such as exposure to extreme heat, vomiting, or intercurrent infections. Particular vigilance is required for changes in fluid and food intake.

Under these conditions, lithium is a safe and effective treatment for the elderly patient.

PSYCHOSTIMULANTS

Methylphenidate is used occasionally to treat patients who experience mild depression with fatigue, slowing of cognitive function, and withdrawn behavior. The drug is also administered to patients who are unable to tolerate standard antidepressants because of medical contraindications or hypersensitivity to toxic effects. When effective, methylphenidate produces a rapid therapeutic response characterized by improvement in mood, energy, and responsivity to surroundings. Cognitive dysfunction that is secondary to depression may also show improvement. However, methylphenidate has several drawbacks that limit its usefulness as an antidepressant. These include a brief duration of stimulant action; a tendency for depression to "rebound" following drug withdrawal; development of tolerance to some of the stimulant effects; and side effects that include insomnia, anorexia, hyperactivity, hypertension, and premature ventricular contractions. In addition, at high dosage levels patients may develop paranoid ideation leading to overt psychosis.

In administering methylphenidate, the dose should not exceed 20 to 30 mg per day, and the drug should be given early in the day so that it is less likely to interfere with sleep. Also, patients should not be treated for more than 3 months and concomitant use of other antidepressants should be avoided. Methylphenidate may interact with tricyclics or MAOIs to increase the risk of serious cardiotoxicity. Methylphenidate may also impair the metabolism of tricyclics, leading to increased tricyclic plasma levels and risk of toxicity.

Other psychostimulants, such as the amphetamines, pemoline, pentylenetetrazol, and pipradol, have not proven to be effective antidepressants for elderly patients.

COMBINATION ANTIDEPRESSANT-ANTIPSYCHOTIC DRUG THERAPY

Depressed patients with agitated, hostile, or delusional behavior are sometimes treated with combined antidepressant-antipsychotic drug therapy. Depending upon the severity of depression and associated symptomatology, the two classes of drugs may be administered concomitantly, or one may be added to the other after a period of time. There is no precise formula for combining antidepressants and antipsychotics, particularly in elderly patients. The relative dose of each drug is dictated by the nature and severity of the disorder, as well as by the patient's tolerance of each medication. As a general rule, drug combinations should be employed only when there is a clear expectation that a single drug will not be effective. Because serious adverse effects, including tardive dyskinesia, are associated with antipsychotic drug use in the elderly, these drugs should be used only when absolutely necessary.

When used in combination, antipsychotic drugs may exert inhibitory effects on the metabolism of tricyclic antidepressants and, in some patients, may increase the tricyclic plasma level and the consequent risk of toxicity. Combined therapy may be particularly troublesome if both the antidepressant and antipsychotic drug have potent anticholinergic effects. Thus, strongly anticholinergic tricyclics, such as amitriptyline, should not be combined with strongly anticholinergic antipyschotics, such as chlorpromazine, chlorprothixene, and thioridazine. Additive anticholinergic effects may lead to paralytic ileus or bladder toxicity, or to confusion, delirium, and anticholinergic psychosis. Where an antipsychotic is necessary, a drug with minimal anticholinergic activity should be chosen, such as perphenazine or haloperidol.

The most popular combination of a tricyclic and an antipsychotic drug is amitriptyline and perphenazine. The combination is commercially available in fixed doses of various combinations of 2 and 4 mg of perphenazine and 10, 25, and 50 mg of amitriptyline. In elderly patients, the unit dose of 4 mg of perphenazine and 10 mg of amitriptyline is administered three to four times a day initially and then adjusted as required. An advantage of this combination is that the anticholinergic effects of amitriptyline may afford protection against the extrapyramidal effects induced by perphenazine. The various dose combinations have also been well tested for interaction effects and toxicity. However, the powerful anticholinergic effects of amitriptyline may pose a serious problem for many aged patients and may actually exacerbate symptomatology, particularly in patients with cognitive deficits. Another drawback of this combination, as well as other combinations, is that it is difficult to know which drug to adjust when toxicity occurs or when the patient fails to show clinical improvement.

Perhaps the most justifiable use of combined antidepressant-antipsychotic drug therapy is the treatment of psychotic or delusional depression. Recent studies suggest that both drugs may be required for effective treatment of such disorders. However, even in these cases, effective single-drug therapy should not be ruled out. For example, amoxapine, a new tricyclic structurally similar to the antipsychotic drug loxapine, is reported to be effective in psychotic depression and may be considered in such patients.

Occasionally, antipsychotic drugs are administered without antidepressants to depressed patients with significant agitation or anxiety. This use of antipsychotic drugs has not been well studied in elderly patients and is recommended only if appropriate antidepressant drug therapy is found to be ineffective or contraindicated.

In summary, then, depression in elderly patients can often be effectively and safely treated with psychotherapeutic drugs. Other alternatives clearly exist, however. Electroconvulsive therapy (ECT), a second form of somatic therapy, will be considered in chapter 6, and two means of nonsomatic intervention will be considered in chapters 7 and 8.

TABLE 1

Side Effect Profiles of Antidepressant Drugs

Generic name	Sedation potency	Potential for cardiovascular toxicity	Anticholinergic potency
Amitriptyline	++	+	++
Amoxapine	++	?	+
Desipramine	–	+	–
Doxepin	++	+	+
Imipramine	+	+	+
Maprotiline	+	–	–
Nomifensine	–	–	–
Nortriptyline	+	+	+
Protriptyline	–	+	+
Trazodone	+++	–	–
Trimipramine	++	+	+

Note. Potency ranges from – (lowest) to +++ (highest).

TABLE 2

Usual Dosage Range of Antidepressants for Elderly Patients

Generic name	Dose (mg/day)
Amitriptyline	50–100
Amoxapine	75–150
Desipramine	25–100
Imipramine	30–100
Maprotiline	50–75
Nortriptyline	30–50
Protriptyline	15–20
Trimipramine	50–100

REFERENCES

1. Hollister, L. E. Interactions of psychotherapeutic drugs with other drugs and disease states. In M. A. Lipton, A. DiMascio, & K. F. Killian (Eds.), *Psychopharmacology: A generation of progress.* New York: Raven Press, 1978, pp. 987-992.

2. Mendels, J. Antidepressants. In T. Crook & G. Cohen (Eds.), *Physician's handbook on psychotherapeutic drug use in the aged.* New Canaan, Conn.: Mark Powley Associates, 1981, pp. 27-36.

3. Prien, R.F., & Gershon, S. Lithium therapy in the elderly. In T. Crook & G. Cohen (Eds.), *Physician's handbook on psychotherapeutic drug use in the aged.* New Canaan, Conn.: Mark Powley Associates, 1981, pp. 27-36.

4. Tyrer, P. Clinical use of monoamine oxidase inhibitors. In E. S. Paykel & A. Coppen (Eds.), *Psychopharmacology of affective disorders.* New York: Oxford University Press, 1979, pp. 159-179.

Dr. Fink is Professor of Psychiatry at the State University of New York Medical School at Stony Brook and Director of the Division of Clinical Sciences at Long Island Research Institute. He is the author of more than 300 publications on such diverse topics as psychopharmacology, electroencephalography, substance abuse, and psycholinguistics. He has published two books and many papers on electroconvulsive therapy and was a member of the American Psychiatric Association's Task Force on Convulsive Therapy. Dr. Fink is a past president of the American Psychopathological Association and has been the recipient of many awards and honors, including the 1979 Anna Monika Foundation Award for his contributions to the study of depression.

Chapter 6

Guidelines for Electroconvulsive Therapy in the Elderly

Max Fink, M.D.

In the treatment of elderly patients with severe endogenous depression, electroconvulsive therapy (ECT) may be as effective or more effective than pharmacotherapy. Also, ECT does not present the cardiovascular and autonomic risks associated with traditional tricyclic antidepressants. However, the treatment may produce adverse effects such as amnesia, it is relatively difficult to administer, it requires special skills and equipment, and the public image of ECT is generally quite negative. Thus, the use of ECT is generally restricted to patients with severe endogenous depression, and often those who have failed to respond to other treatments. In such patients, the effects of ECT may be dramatic and, at times, lifesaving.

INDICATIONS

Treatment with ECT generally requires four to eight seizures given twice or three times per week. In deciding whether to recommend ECT, the physician must consider a number of factors, including the nature and severity of the depressive disorder, the probability of response and risks associated with other forms of therapy, and the likely benefits and risks of ECT. In addition to the risk of amnesia and those associated with anesthesia used in the procedure, the social stigma of having had ECT must be considered.

FIGURE 1

Decision Flow Chart for the Use of Electroconvulsive Therapy (ECT) in the Elderly Patient

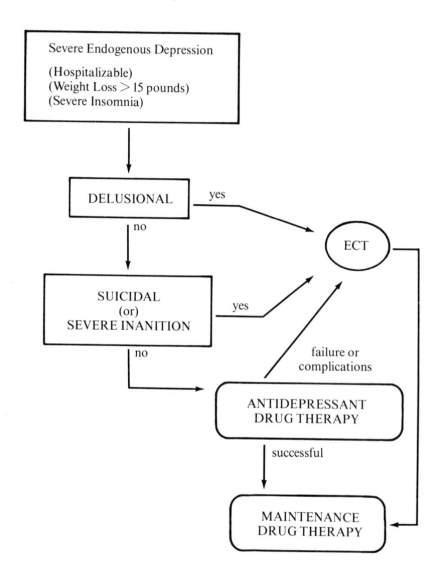

In general, ECT is reserved for patients in whom depression is serious enough to warrant hospitalization. The technique is particularly effective in patients who display a predominance of somatic symptoms, such as insomnia, anorexia, and decreased libido. As noted in chapter 1, delusional patients are often treatment resistant and they, too, frequently respond to ECT. In the case of suicidal patients or those who refuse food and are cachectic, ECT is clearly indicated. These considerations are shown schematically in Figure 1.

In view of the cardiovascular and autonomic effects associated with tricyclic antidepressants and monoamine oxidase inhibitors, it can be argued that psychotic patients with renal, cardiac, or hepatic decompensation, or recent coronary occlusion, are suitable candidates for ECT. Although each seizure in ECT is physically demanding—raising blood pressure and stimulating arrhythmia and tachycardia—the incidence of cardiovascular complications is low, even in patients who have had a recent myocardial infarction. In fact, patients with cardiac pacemakers have been treated successfully with ECT. On balance, for severely depressed patients with certain severe, specific medical conditions, ECT may at times be safer than traditional antidepressant drug regimens.

DRUGS AND ECT

Studies in depressed young adults have found that no advantage is gained by combining traditional antidepressant drug therapy with ECT. On the contrary, the anticholinergic and autonomic effects of the traditional antidepressant drugs increase the risks of complications in ECT. The combined use of ECT and psychotropic drugs (including lithium) may be associated with an increased incidence of organic psychoses. It is a reasonable conclusion that such combined therapy should not ordinarily be attempted with elderly patients.

What of ECT in patients who require maintenance medication for medical conditions? In such instances, attention should be directed to the potential interactions of the drugs with the ECT seizure and with the anesthetic agents used in the procedure. This is particularly true for cardiovascular drugs, such as lidocaine, quinidine, digitalis, and some diuretics. These compounds may interact with succinylcholine to produce a prolonged respiratory paralysis, arrhythmia, or cardiac arrest. It is also true for lithium, where the combination with succinylcholine may lead to prolongation of respiratory effects.

While the combined use of ECT and antidepressant medication does not appear advisable, administration of antidepressants following a course of ECT may help sustain clinical improvement.

RISK-BENEFIT ANALYSIS

Prior to the mid-1950s, ECT treatments were unmodified by anesthesia and muscle relaxants, and consent was often informal. Also, because the psychotropic drugs upon which we now depend so heavily had not been introduced, ECT was administered in many psychiatric disorders. With the introduction of anesthesia and succinylcholine in the mid-1950s, the mode of ECT induction changed considerably, and with it the risks and untoward consequences. Modern ECT methods use barbiturate anesthesia, unilateral electrode placement, low induction currents, hyperoxygenation, and seizure monitoring. Concomitant drugs are restricted to those substances necessary for medical disorders. It is important for the physician referring an elderly patient for ECT to assure that treatments are given by therapists who employ modern methods, in settings where facilities are available to deal with treatment complications.

A major concern with ECT in all age groups that may be further exaggerated in aged patients, particularly those with mild to moderate cognitive impairment, is memory loss following treatment. This problem can be mitigated by unilateral electrode placement, but memory loss remains a valid concern. However, in the elderly patient suffering from a life threatening or disabling psychotic depressive disorder, such a risk must be balanced against the often clear, and sometimes dramatic, benefits of ECT.

The next chapter turns to the treatment of less severely depressed, nonendogenous patients, and from somatic to nonsomatic interventions.

REFERENCES

1. Bigger, T. G. Electroconvulsive therapy in the medically ill patient. *Psychiatric Clinics of North America*, 1981, *4*, 391-405.

2. Fink, M. *Convulsive therapy: Theory and practice.* New York: Raven Press, 1979.

3. Fink, M. ECT in the elderly. In C. Eisdorfer & W. Fann (Eds.), *Treatment of psychopathology in the aged.* New York: Springer Verlag, in press.

Dr. Wolpe is Professor of Psychiatry and Director of the Behavior Therapy Unit at Temple University School of Medicine in Philadelphia. He is widely regarded as the father of behavior therapy and is the recipient of many honors and awards, including the American Psychological Association's 1979 Distinguished Scientific Award for Applications of Psychology.

Chapter 7

Behavior Therapy for the Primary Care Physician

Joseph Wolpe, M.D.

In behavior therapy, experimentally established principles of learning are applied to change maladaptive emotional habits. The habits that are the most frequent targets, and the core of neuroses, are inappropriate anxiety reactions. These are learned reactions and are generally responsive to behavior therapy.

In elderly patients, as in younger adults, many depressions are secondary to neurotic anxiety and, thus, can be successfully treated by the physician using the techniques of behavior therapy. This chapter will provide guidelines for identifying patients responsive to behavior therapy and describe behavioral methods that may be applied by the general practitioner.

IDENTIFYING APPROPRIATE PATIENTS

Behavior therapy is appropriate in nonendogenous, unipolar depressions in which a significant component of anxiety is present. These patients may appear, or report feeling, nervous, jittery, fearful, apprehensive, or panicky in certain circumstances. Muscular and autonomic signs of anxiety — such as trembling, restlessness, tachycardia, or sweating — may accompany the symptoms of depression. Depression and anxiety frequently coexist in aged patients, as in young adults, and as noted in chapter 1, the diagnostic distinction between the two conditions may be difficult. In many cases the symptoms of depression are secondary to anxiety and will diminish when the anxiety is treated.

Behavior therapy is not appropriate in unipolar endogenous depression or in bipolar depression; appropriate treatment strategies for those conditions are described in chapters 5 and 6. The discussion of cognitive therapy in chapter 8 is appropriate to both unipolar endogenous and nonendogenous patients in whom negative distortions of reality and cognitive errors underlie depression.

BASIC TREATMENT PROCEDURES

Eliciting Factors That Trigger Anxiety

The initial step in any anxiety-eliminating procedure is identification of factors that are associated with and that trigger the anxiety. In most cases anxiety is automatically triggered by certain events or in certain circumstances, although the patient is intellectually aware that he or she is in no danger. Thus, patients cannot be "talked" out of their anxiety, and their emotional state will not be altered through rational argument. For example, a patient may feel anxious in an elevator, at the sight of a bloodstained bandage, or at being the center of attention in a living room, even though it is perfectly clear that no harm will come from any of these circumstances.

The physician can elicit factors that trigger anxiety by carefully questioning the patient about the conditions under which anxiety arises. If a patient states that he or she is always anxious to a greater or lesser extent, questioning should focus on factors that make the condition worse. In depression associated with anxiety, social triggers are most frequently seen; that is, the patient is made anxious by the behavior of other people. The intensity of the anxiety generally varies depending upon the type of "hostile" behavior and the identity of the person displaying hostility. For example, a particular elderly patient may become quite anxious at being thought foolish, less anxious at being thought selfish, and not at all anxious at being thought stubborn or contentious. Similarly, hostility from a spouse may be quite anxiety arousing, while the same actions may be progressively less upsetting when exhibited by an adult child, sibling, close friend, and remote acquaintance, in that order. After carefully eliciting information about the conditions under which a patient becomes anxious, it is the task of the physician to construct a list in which events are ranked according to their anxiety-eliciting potential.

Teaching Relaxation

The next step in behavior therapy is to teach patients to calm themselves by relaxing. The deep relaxation that must be taught is different from what is ordinarily referred to as "relaxing," that is, those feelings associated with lying in bed, basking in the sun, or taking a hot bath. Deep relaxation is achieved by directly working on the muscles. The patient is taught to locate, one at a time, the muscles in various body zones — forehead, lower face, jaws, neck, shoulders, arms, thighs, and legs. These muscle groups are located by following instructions from the physician to contract them. For example, one group of forehead muscles is located by raising the eyebrows and another is located by frowning; similarly, jaw muscles are located by biting on the teeth. Immediately after tensing a muscle, the patient is shown how to let it go and *keep on letting go*. Through this action, the patient can get beyond the point that he or she would ordinarily think of as "relaxed." When the patient learns to relax muscles beyond their normal resting state, he or she will be able to bring about antianxiety autonomic responses. For example, pulse rate will be reduced, breathing will become slower and more regular, and the palms will become less moist. These autonomic effects become increasingly marked with practice. The patient should be instructed to practice this relaxation technique twice each day, in 15-minute periods. Patients will learn to recognize when they have succeeded in relaxing by experiencing such resultant feelings as warmth, heaviness, and paresthesia in the limbs and elsewhere.

Systematic Desensitization

When anxiety sources have been defined and ranked and the patient has been taught to become calm through relaxing, the physician is ready to begin systematic desensitization, the most effective technique for overcoming anxiety. The patient, sitting comfortably, is asked to close his or her eyes. The physician then tells the patient to relax in the way that he or she has practiced, and directs the patient's attention to each muscle group in turn, starting from the face and moving downward.

Two or three minutes after the relaxation instructions have concluded, the physician checks the patient's emotional state. If a patient reports feeling calm, he or she is asked to imagine the least disturbing of the anxiety-arousing situations on the list previously constructed. For example, a patient sensitive to criticism might first be asked to imagine overhearing a distant acquaintance describing him or her as untidy. As a rule, even this "weak" scene will break into the calmness and arouse a little anxiety. Two or three repetitions of the scene, each of a few seconds' duration, will reduce the anxiety to zero, at which point the next "stronger" scene can be similarly treated. After a number of such steps, varying according to the content of the information obtained, even the "strongest" scene will totally lose its capacity to arouse anxiety.

Another example is provided by the patient who becomes anxious at being the center of attention in social situations. The patient is likely to have minimal anxiety before a small audience and become increasingly anxious as the audience increases in size. In this case, the physician determines the relationship between size of audience and anxiety in advance. If a particular patient has minimal anxiety in the presence of two strangers, he or she is made as calm as possible through relaxation, and then asked briefly to imagine being confronted by two strangers. The small amount of anxiety this image arouses will diminish to zero after about three presentations. Then images are presented that involve, in turn, 5, 7, 10, 15, 20, 30 people and so on, until the highest number likely to be encountered in reality fails to arouse anxiety.

All of this will take several sessions to achieve. What is of greatest importance is that between sessions, the patient will find that anxiety is greatly diminished in corresponding real-life situations and, if the anxiety is the basis of a depression, the depression, too, will progressively recede. As a matter of fact, depression very often ceases to be a problem well before the treatment of anxiety has been completed.

Other Behavioral Techniques

At times, behavioral therapy techniques other than systematic desensitization will be indicated. For example, depression in the elderly patient may be the result of a sense of helplessness when the patient, because of neurotic timidity, is repeatedly taken advantage of by others. In such a case, assertiveness training is indicated. This may involve no more than instructing the patient that it is appropriate to say "no" to an unreasonable demand. When patients are taught to use socially appropriate means of expressing anger and other feelings, the fear that previously inhibited them often declines, and with it their depressive symptoms.

A useful technique is the "I statement." This is a technique by which the depressed elderly patient can be taught to express his or her feelings while avoiding recrimination. The patient is taught to respond to infringements by others with the statement, "When you do _____, I feel _____." For example, "When you fail to call me on Mother's Day, I feel rejected." In this example, if the statement is made in a firm but friendly manner and not tearfully, it may motivate children to attend to the feelings of the aged parent. Such elementary techniques of assertiveness often help the patient overcome anxiety associated with expressing feelings and counteract the feelings of helplessness associated with depression.

Another source of anxiety frequently overlooked in the depressed patient is simply misinformation. For example, elderly patients may be anxious and, consequently, depressed, because they fear they are the victim of a terminal illness, or that a social catastrophe predicted by a doomsday prophet is imminent. In such cases, effective therapy may consist of simply providing the patient with corrective information. In some patients, in whom depression is related to cognitive distortions, the techniques described in the following chapter will also be found extremely useful.

For a concise jargon-free exposition of the principles, practices and range of applications of behavior therapy, the reader is referred to the publication referenced below.

REFERENCE

1. Wolpe, J., & Wolpe, D. *Our useless fears.* Boston, Mass.: Houghton Mifflin, 1981.

Dr. Emery is Director of the Los Angeles Center for Cognitive Therapy and Assistant Professor of Psychology at the University of California, Los Angeles. He was formerly on the medical faculty at the University of Pennsylvania where he worked with Dr. Aaron T. Beck to develop the techniques of cognitive therapy. Dr. Emery has published widely on the application of cognitive therapy principles to different psychiatric and behavioral problems, including depression in the elderly.

Chapter 8

Cognitive Therapy of Depression in the Elderly

Gary Emery, Ph.D.

Cognitive therapists believe that depression is essentially a thinking disorder. The cognitive model holds that a person's thoughts and ideas determine how he or she feels and acts. Thus, when patients believe they have been rejected and abandoned (whether they have been or not), they feel sad and lonely. When they believe they have done something unforgivable, they feel guilty. When they think life is too difficult, they become apathetic and withdrawn. When they think there is no solution to their problems, they may believe suicide is the only way out. Depressed individuals distort experiences to agree with their negative view of themselves and of the world. As they become more depressed, they use the symptoms of their depression as further proof that they are worthless, and a vicious downward spiral develops.

Many writers have noted that depressed older individuals are consumed with negative ideas about themselves ("I've been a failure my whole life"), about the world ("No one wants to be around old people"), and about the future ("Things will never get better, only worse"). The relationship between distorted negative thoughts and depression is compounded in the elderly because of age stereotypes. Many of the symptoms of depression, such as apathy, loss of memory and concentration, withdrawal, and increased dependency, also characterize stereotypes of aging. Friends and relatives of the depressed elderly patient often mistakenly assume the symptoms of depression are inevitable signs of aging and, as a result, they may reinforce the older patient's mistaken notions.

Physicians, including busy primary care physicians, can work with depressed older patients in a number of ways to help them identify and correct their cognitive distortions. An active and direct approach is best. Patients can be told that their symptoms should be seen as problems to be solved, not as permanent traits. Physicians can convey to patients the message that they can learn to master the problems they consider insurmountable by reevaluating their thinking.

In many cases, negative thoughts that lead to depression can be corrected by simply providing information about the disorder. Many older people falsely attribute the symptoms of their depression to aging or to physical causes. This error can be corrected by strongly and repeatedly distinguishing between symptoms of depression and changes associated with normal aging. For example, loss of sexual desire is a common symptom of depression, but in older men the loss may be seen as permanent and may be attributed to age. Patients can be informed that this is a symptom of depression and that research has shown the majority of men to have active sex lives up to the 75th year and, in many cases, into the 80s and beyond.

Simply presenting depression as a problem of faulty thinking often provides relief to older patients. One must be aware, however, that many older people are sensitive to criticism about their thinking ability. For this reason, the physician has to assure patients that this type of faulty thinking is due to depression and not to aging.

DEALING WITH THE BEHAVIORAL
SYMPTOMS OF DEPRESSION

The first symptoms of depression usually targeted for change are the behavioral symptoms, including social withdrawal, apathy, and passive behavior. The goal is to help patients become more active.

Encouraging Therapeutic Activities

The physician can help motivate the patient by pointing out the advantages of becoming more active. These include:

1. Activity changes one's thinking—activity shows the patient that he or she can start and finish projects.
2. Activity improves mood—patients will be less depressed when active or when they have completed an activity.
3. Activity counteracts the fatigue found in depression—activity actually improves, rather than diminishes, the patient's physical and mental energy reserves.
4. Activity increases motivation—in depression, motivation works backwards; the patient has to do what he doesn't feel like doing before he wants to do it.
5. Activity improves mental ability—solutions to what appear to be insoluble problems come to mind after the patient begins moving.
6. Activity improves relationships with others—family members and others will respond in a positive manner to the patient's attempts to be more active.

In helping the patient become more active, the physician first suggests that activities be broken down into small, manageable steps. Patients should first attempt activities that are not too difficult: for example, cleaning one room in a house, calling a friend, getting a car serviced, or buying one article of clothing. As they progress to more complex and difficult undertakings, patients should be encouraged to break each task down into a series of small manageable tasks.

Depressed patients, however, often do not believe they are capable of carrying out even the simplest tasks. The physician can counteract this by using the idea of *behavioral experiments.* In this procedure the patient's negative predictions about tasks to be performed are elicited ("It's too hard," "I don't think I can do it," "I won't enjoy it"). The physician then suggests that the patient conduct an experiment to see if his or her thoughts are true. The experiments should be set up as "no lose" situations. If patients cannot complete the tasks, this information can be used in planning other tasks. Success in behavioral experiments usually sparks a patient's interest and frequently exerts an immediate therapeutic effect by discouraging such negative thoughts as "I am ineffective," "I can't do anything right," and "I don't enjoy anything."

In encouraging increased activity, it is important to emphasize the need to schedule activities. Patients should be encouraged to schedule activities similar to what they enjoyed doing before they became depressed. For example, the older person who enjoyed social activities may be encouraged to phone or call on friends, go to meetings, or join groups. The person who was action oriented, perhaps as an executive, may be encouraged to plan activities that involve a sense of mastery, such as completing jobs around the house. The physician may actually review the patient's weekly schedule or convey to the patient's family the importance of scheduling and attempt to enlist their help.

Following are guidelines the physician can use to help the patient schedule activities.

1. Plan with flexibility — the schedule should be used as a guide.

2. Build in alternatives — if a scheduled activity must be canceled, an alternative should be available.

3. Stick with the general plan — if the patient finishes an activity earlier than planned, do not have him or her begin the next scheduled activity. Rather, have the patient do something pleasurable with the extra time.

4. Schedule activities in one-hour and half-hour intervals — do not plan activities that are either too specific or too general. Try for something in between such as "Go to bank, eat lunch at shopping mall, go to cleaners."

5. Avoid performance appraisals — patients should write down what they are going to do, not how much or how well they're going to do it.

6. After completing a scheduled day, the patient should write down what he or she did — this activity often provides a sense of mastery and helps in scheduling activities for the following day.

7. Be task oriented — concentrate on following the schedule and not on getting over depression. By working on activity, the patient will eventually feel better.

The depressed person will typically have only partial success in following the schedule of activities and will often be self-critical. The physician can warn the patient in advance that this may happen and use the perceived failure to advantage by having the patient write down self-critical thoughts, and thoughts that stop him or her from taking action. When these thoughts are written down, they can be looked at in more realistic ways, as discussed in the following section.

Minimizing Unpleasant Activities

The physician can also help the depressed patient control negative feelings by showing him or her how to avoid or minimize unpleasant activities. Following are some methods the patient can use.

1. Avoid the situation — a surprising number of activities regarded by the aged depressed patient as unpleasant can simply be avoided. For example, patients who complain that they become depressed when lying in bed at night unable to sleep should be advised to get out of bed and read, listen to music, or undertake crossword puzzles or some other activity until they become tired. The patient may also be advised against daytime naps and so on.

2. Change the situation — most elderly depressed patients feel helpless and lack a sense of mastery over their environment. The physician can encourage a sense of mastery by providing the patient with specific means of changing unpleasant situations. For example, the bored patient may pursue volunteer activities, the housebound patient may explore community transportation programs, or the patient living in an unpleasant setting can explore available alternatives.

3. Plan — good planning can prevent many unpleasant events such as being behind in paperwork or financial obligations.

4. Say "no" — older people can avoid many unpleasant activities by being more assertive. As discussed in chapter 7, it is often therapeutic for the physician to simply indicate that it is acceptable and desirable for the patient to convey his or her thoughts and feelings clearly to others. For example, it is appropriate to decline a request to babysit or to request a late visitor to leave.

5. Master the problem — the patient can move toward the problem and learn how to do tasks he or she has been avoiding. Tasks that seem insurmountable can frequently be conquered when broken down into small steps.

DEALING WITH THE EMOTIONAL
SYMPTOMS OF DEPRESSION

The physician can help patients learn to control their negative feelings by showing them how they can correct their erroneous thinking. Patients are instructed that all feelings are caused by thoughts that precede them. Often these thoughts are fleeting and occur automatically, so that the patient is not even aware of them. Patients must be instructed to identify and record their thoughts each time a negative feeling occurs. One method is the two-column technique in which patients write down the thoughts that precede their negative feelings in one column and then develop more realistic alternatives to their thoughts and record them in the opposite column. Table 1 provides examples of common thinking errors of depressed patients and some realistic alternatives.

Patients can be helped to develop alternatives to their negative thoughts by careful questioning of the reasoning behind each thought. Patients should then be encouraged to question and test the reality of their own thoughts. Table 2 provides 20 questions patients can use to check the relationship of their thoughts to reality.

The three most important questions are

1. What's the evidence that the thought is true? For example, the thought, "My children don't love me" should be looked at objectively. What is the evidence for and against?

2. What's another way of looking at it? For example, inattention from children can be looked at as evidence that "They don't love me" or "They're busy with their own lives."

3. Even if it is true, how bad are the consequences? For example, the patient may see that "Even if they don't love me, I can still choose to be happy." Typically, the depressed elderly patient will use the thought "My children don't love me" as evidence that "I'm no good, I don't deserve their love" and beyond that, "I don't deserve anything."

In addition to answering their negative and distorted thoughts, patients need to act on the new, more realistic thoughts they develop as alternatives. By acting on their new thoughts, patients not only come to believe them intellectually, but emotionally as well. Table 3 provides some ways that patients can act on their new thoughts.

Whenever possible, patients should be encouraged to directly test their beliefs against reality. The physician can help devise such reality tests in the office. For example, many depressed older patients believe they have serious problems with concentration, understanding, and memory. In fact, a number of studies have shown that complaints of memory dysfunction in the elderly are often more closely associated with depression than with actual impairment. To test the reality of such thoughts, the physician can ask the patient to read a paragraph or two from a newspaper or popular magazine and paraphrase what he or she has read. A simple vocabulary test can also be administered, since abilities measured by such a test decline very little with age. It is important to assure that such reality tests are constructed as "no lose" experiments and that the discrepancy between a patient's predicted performance and actual performance is explicitly pointed out. Such actual tests of negative thoughts frequently lead to modification of the thoughts and significant, sometimes dramatic, changes in mood.

THERAPY OUTSIDE THE OFFICE

Obviously, the primary care physician has a very limited amount of time to act as therapist. The patient can be guided using the principles outlined, but most of the therapeutic work must be done outside the office. In fact, even when the therapist is a psychiatrist or psychologist, the most important aspect of cognitive therapy is getting patients to do the "homework" between office visits.

If the patient is severely depressed, this homework should be almost entirely behavioral, aimed at increasing the patient's level of activity. If the patient is less severely depressed, or as the severely depressed patient improves, the physician should encourage use of the two-column technique to identify and answer negative thoughts. At this time the patient should also be encouraged to attempt behavioral "experiments" relevant to his or her problems. For example, the physician may suggest that the patient call two other people during the week "and see whether it makes you feel better or not." Physicians should go out of their way in seeing patients on subsequent visits after introducing the concept of "homework" to inquire as to precisely what has been done, and to reinforce efforts at self-therapy.

As discussed in chapter 4, it is important to consider the patient's family in planning and managing treatment. Thus, it is advantageous to explain cognitive principles to the family as well as to the patient and to enlist the help of the family in homework. Because the patient's depression is likely to have a significant impact on other family members, it may be that they will be able to apply cognitive principles in their own lives, ultimately to the patient's benefit as well as their own. As noted in chapters 3 and 4, however, the physician must be cautious so as not to deprive patients of the opportunity to gain control over important aspects of their feelings and, ultimately, their lives.

The physician must bear in mind at all times that patients do not want to be depressed; rather, they lack the tools to effectively deal with depression. The physician, by using the methods of cognitive therapy, can help provide these tools to the elderly depressed patient.

REFERENCES

1. Beck, A., Rush, J., Shaw, B., & Emery, G. *Cognitive therapy of depression.* New York: Guilford Press, 1979.

2. Emery, G. *A new beginning: How you can change your life through cognitive therapy.* New York: Simon & Schuster, 1981.

Dr. Kastenbaum is Director of the
Adult Development and Aging Program at Arizona State University in
Tempe. He was formerly Superinten-
dent of Cushing Hospital for the Aged in
Framingham, Massachusetts and Professor of Psychology at the University
of Massachusetts. He has published
very extensively in gerontology and on
the topic of death and dying. Dr. Kastenbaum has served as President of the
American Association of Suicidology
and President of the Division of Adult
Development and Aging, American
Psychological Association. He is currently Chair-Elect of the Division of
Behavioral and Social Sciences of the
Gerontological Society.

Chapter 9

Suicidality in the Aged

Robert Kastenbaum, Ph.D.

An intimate relationship exists between depression and suicide in all age groups, but physicians must be particularly alert to the danger of suicide in the depressed elderly patient. The suicide rate among elderly white males is higher than in any other segment of the population and older people, in general, have a far higher proportion of lethal outcomes when a suicide attempt is made than do young adults.

In identifying suicidal aged patients, the physician cannot rely upon a history of previous attempts, although that remains useful information, or a history of psychiatric illness. Some people toy with the idea of suicide for many years, but never act on it or arouse the alarm of their associates. Faced eventually with age-related illness, loss, and stress, they may exercise what they consider to be their last option, and do so with a minimum of advance notice. This differs from the most typical pattern exhibited by younger people, whose words and actions can often be read as a "cry for help." The older person who is contemplating suicide is less likely to announce his or her intentions, although this does happen at times. Nevertheless, it is possible to read the warning signs of suicide in older adults.

The depressed older person often will choose to see a physician if he or she decides to seek any type of professional help and, as noted in chapter 1, the presenting complaint is frequently of a physical rather than emotional problem. Exploration of the physical complaint often provides an opportunity to assess suicidality.

For some people the physical complaint has a meaning beyond itself. The subjective interpretation is that "I am helpless now; I am no good for anything." This attitude can lead to constriction of lifestyle, failure to act in one's own self-interest (as by following a medical regime), and heightened suicidality. "I'm not a man anymore" and "What can I do about it?" are illustrative of the ways in which this attitude is verbalized. "Nobody needs (or wants) me anymore" is a somewhat more typical expression from older women. The physician should look for statements that express the perceived inability to do anything about one's own situation, or to function in a manner consistent with one's self-image. Such statements may not be forthcoming immediately, but may be elicited when the physician inquires about the consequences and implications of the physical complaint. Examples of gentle questions that may encourage the elderly individual to open up are "How has this affected your life?"; "How have you been adjusting to this problem?"; and "Has this interfered with your social life?"

It is important for the physician to refrain from assuming that there is a predictable and "rational" relationship between the objective severity of the physical complaint and the subjective response. A serious, even life-threatening, condition does not necessarily result in heightened suicidality or a sense of helplessness. The observer might think to himself, "If I were in his shoes, I'm not sure I'd want to go on." This would be a premature and often an incorrect conclusion. Some people are virtually "suicide proof," and still others have successful ways of coping with debilitation. Conversely, in other individuals a relatively minor physical complaint can be perceived as devastating and lead to either a passive withdrawal from life or overt suicidal behavior. A person who has taken pride in being independent may feel humiliated at having to depend on others as a result of physical impairment and may think of suicide as "the one thing I can still do for myself." The more the physician can learn about the patient's distinctive life-style and values, the better perspective he or she will have in evaluating the likely effect of the physical disorder. One elderly man with a strong "macho" self-image, for example, may turn against himself if he can no longer project this image convincingly, whereas another man will be more seriously shaken by an occasional lapse of memory. Particular care should be taken when the patient functions within an ethnic life-style that is not intimately familiar to the physician. Pain and discomfort may disorganize one person, whereas another may accept distress as a burden to be borne without complaint.

In exploring the patient's attitude toward the physical complaint, it is sometimes helpful to ask, "Have you ever known anybody who has the same kind of trouble you have?" Through this approach the physician will sometimes learn of past experiences that strongly influence the patient's attitude toward his or her illness. Such factors include misinformation about the etiology or outcome, such as comparing oneself with someone else whose condition and prognosis were really not the same. Suicidality can be triggered by the judgment that one now has "what did old Mr. Cooper in" and, therefore, there is nothing to be done about it.

Another line of questioning worth pursuing concerns the patient's anticipations of what is likely to happen next. Questions may include "What do you think will come of this condition?" and "How do you see yourself a month (a year) from now?" Anticipations of dreaded events are another source of suicidality. This is especially true for individuals who keep their thoughts and feelings to themselves, either because of their introversive nature or because they lack companions with whom to share such concerns. In such instances, anticipations of terrible things that might be in prospect tend to feed on themselves and become a more powerful factor in suicidality than is the present state of the physical complaint. The patient who refuses to think of the future at all, or characterizes it as bleak and foreboding is at increased risk for suicide. In eliciting thoughts about the future, and helping the patient develop a more constructive attitude, it is sometimes helpful to ask, "What is the worst that you think might happen?" followed by "How would you bear that, if it came to pass?"

A sensitive exploration of recent losses is highly recommended. Some elderly depressed people approach the physician with their physical complaints only and may not mention significant losses unless specifically asked. Thoughts of suicide may accompany depression following the death of a spouse of many years or another family member or close friend. A recent bereavement may bring back earlier losses whose weight is added to the present sorrow and anxiety. It is not uncommon, for example, that a recent bereavement will lead an elderly person to once again experience the feelings aroused by the death of his or her mother or father many years ago.

In exploring the patient's response to bereavement, it is useful to watch for indications of a wish to "join" the deceased. "My life is nothing without him" and "He wants me to be with him" illustrate an attitude that can generate suicidal action. Many bereaved people have a strong sense of yearning for the lost one and a sense of the deceased's presence. This does not always indicate suicidal potential, but does suggest that further exploration is warranted. It is important to learn what importance is attached to this loss and how the patient has handled losses in the past, although it must be borne in mind that strategies for handling past losses may no longer be available. For example, the man who formerly threw himself into his work for distraction may no longer be able to do so because he has retired from the workplace.

The physician should also be alert to clues of suicidality in the behavior of the depressed elderly patient. For example, a change from agitated to quiet depression should be regarded as a danger signal rather than as improvement. Although some people attempt suicide in a state of panic, others show a calmer, more detached attitude not long before they attempt to take their lives. This sometimes reflects the mentally soothing effect of having made a decision after a period of turmoil and uncertainty. When such a clinical change is observed, the physician should indicate to the patient that he or she is aware that something is going on. This can generally be accomplished by questions such as, "You have a different look about you today, Mr. Jones — am I right?" Such questions will sometimes reveal a detailed suicidal plan.

Whenever the patient indicates that he or she has contemplated suicide, an attempt should be made to determine whether concrete preparatory actions have been taken, such as stockpiling drugs and selecting a time and place. The existence of a concrete, fully developed plan for suicide calls for intervention by the physician. This may require enlisting the help of family members or community services, as discussed in chapters 3 and 4.

Among the constructive actions the physician may take in dealing with potentially suicidal depressed patients are the following:

1. Establish a sense of concern for the patient's welfare through subtle gestures such as direct eye contact, touch, tone of voice, and through a willingness to listen. Use any available technique to counter the patient's thoughts of personal worthlessness.

2. Use both the behavioral and cognitive techniques outlined in chapter 8. For example, help the patient schedule activities that will distract him or her from suicidal ideation and provide structure and direction in daily life. Use cognitive techniques to examine the accuracy of suicidal thoughts. For example, examine the validity of such thoughts as "I might as well be dead and no one would care," or "I am no good to anyone." Indicate that suicidal thoughts are symptoms of depression, rather than rational ideas, and that they will diminish as the depression clears.

3. Provide accurate information to help counteract the patient's feelings of hopelessness and fear about the future. For example, indicate that depression can usually be treated successfully and that the patient's current distress will not be unremitting.

4. Do what you can to have the patient surrender any cache of medications he or she may have been using or accumulating, and exercise caution in making drugs the primary treatment modality. Although there is a place for antidepressant medication in the treatment plan, drugs should always be used within a broader context of understanding and assistance. The depressed patient may otherwise come to feel that he or she is being given a drug rather than the attention of a doctor, and this may further strengthen the sense of worthlessness.

5. Enlist the help of the patient's family and other available community resources, as discussed in chapters 3 and 4.

6. Mental hospitalization for suicidal risk is often more convenient than it is useful. In some instances there is the danger of starting a process that will convert a troubled person into a "geriatric patient" and lead to a humiliating and depressing discontinuity in the patient's life. Even more important, suicide will remain a possibility — in or out of the institution—unless something useful is done about the situation that generated the self-destructive inclination or the individual's manner of responding to it. A change of living arrangement may at times be indicated, but this does not necessarily mean mental hospitalization which, in any event, should seldom be envisioned as a permanent solution.

One final point is worth bearing in mind. The old person who is depressed and suicidal today does not have to be depressed and suicidal tomorrow. The negative assumptions once held by many healthcare professionals are rapidly giving way to positive experiences now that more physicians and others have taken up the challenge of offering the elderly the best of their knowledge and skills.

REFERENCES

1. Farberow, N. L. (Ed.). *The many faces of suicide.* New York: McGraw-Hill, 1980.

2. Kastenbaum, R. The physician and the terminally ill person. In I. Rossman (Ed.), *Clinical Geriatrics* (2nd ed.). Philadelphia: Lippincott, 1979, 576–591.

CIBA

Apresoline® hydrochloride
(hydralazine hydrochloride USP)

TABLETS

INDICATIONS
Essential hypertension, alone or as an adjunct.

CONTRAINDICATIONS
Hypersensitivity to hydralazine; coronary artery disease; and mitral valvular rheumatic heart disease.

WARNINGS
Hydralazine may produce in a few patients a clinical picture simulating systemic lupus erythematosus. In such patients hydralazine should be discontinued unless the benefit-to-risk determination requires continued antihypertensive therapy with this drug. Symptoms and signs usually regress when the drug is discontinued but residua have been detected many years later. Long-term treatment with steroids may be necessary.

Complete blood counts, L. E. cell preparations, and antinuclear antibody titer determinations are indicated before and periodically during prolonged therapy with hydralazine even though the patient is asymptomatic. These studies are also indicated if the patient develops arthralgia, fever, chest pain, continued malaise or other unexplained signs or symptoms.

A positive antinuclear antibody titer and/or positive L. E. cell reaction requires that the physician carefully weigh the implications of the test results against the benefits to be derived from antihypertensive therapy with hydralazine.

Use MAO inhibitors with caution in patients receiving hydralazine.

When other potent parenteral antihypertensive drugs, such as diazoxide, are used in combination with hydralazine, patients should be continuously observed for several hours for any excessive fall in blood pressure. Profound hypotensive episodes may occur when diazoxide injection and Apresoline (hydralazine hydrochloride) are used concomitantly.

Usage in Pregnancy
Animal studies indicate that hydralazine is teratogenic in mice, possibly in rabbits, and not in rats. Teratogenic effects observed were cleft palate and malformations of facial and cranial bones. Although clinical experience does not include any positive evidence of adverse effects on the human fetus, hydralazine should not be used during pregnancy unless the expected benefit clearly justifies the potential risk to the fetus.

PRECAUTIONS
Myocardial stimulation produced by Apresoline can cause anginal attacks and ECG changes of myocardial ischemia. The drug has been implicated in the production of myocardial infarction. It must, therefore, be used with caution in patients with suspected coronary artery disease.

The "hyperdynamic" circulation caused by Apresoline may accentuate specific cardiovascular inadequacies. An example is that Apresoline may increase pulmonary artery pressure in patients with mitral valvular disease. The drug may reduce the pressor responses to epinephrine. Postural hypotension may result from Apresoline, but is less common than with ganglionic blocking agents. Use with caution in patients with cerebral vascular accidents.

In hypertensive patients with normal kidneys who are treated with Apresoline, there is evidence of increased renal blood flow and a maintenance of glomerular filtration rate. In some instances improved renal function has been noted where control values were below normal prior to Apresoline administration. However, as with any antihypertensive agent, Apresoline should be used with caution in patients with advanced renal damage.

Peripheral neuritis, evidenced by paresthesias, numbness, and tingling, has been observed. Published evidence suggests an antipyridoxine effect and the addition of pyridoxine to the regimen if symptoms develop.

Blood dyscrasias, consisting of reduction in hemoglobin and red cell count, leukopenia, agranulocytosis, and purpura, have been reported. If such abnormalities develop, discontinue therapy. Periodic blood counts are advised during prolonged therapy.

The Apresoline tablets (10 and 100 mg) contain FD&C Yellow No. 5 (tartrazine) which may cause allergic-type reactions (including bronchial asthma) in certain susceptible individuals. Although the overall incidence of FD&C Yellow No. 5 (tartrazine) sensitivity in the general population is low, it is frequently seen in patients who also have aspirin hypersensitivity.

ADVERSE REACTIONS
Adverse reactions with Apresoline are usually reversible when dosage is reduced. However, in some cases it may be necessary to discontinue the drug.

Common: Headache; palpitations; anorexia; nausea; vomiting; diarrhea; tachycardia; angina pectoris.

Less Frequent: Nasal congestion; flushing; lacrimation; conjunctivitis; peripheral neuritis, evidenced by paresthesias, numbness, and tingling; edema; dizziness; tremors; muscle cramps; psychotic reactions characterized by depression, disorientation, or anxiety; hypersensitivity (including rash, urticaria, pruritus, fever, chills, arthralgia, eosinophilia, and, rarely, hepatitis); constipation; difficulty in micturition; dyspnea; paralytic ileus; lymphadenopathy; splenomegaly; blood dyscrasias, consisting of reduction in hemoglobin and red cell count, leukopenia, agranulocytosis, and purpura; hypotension; paradoxical pressor response.

DOSAGE AND ADMINISTRATION
Initiate therapy in gradually increasing dosages; adjust according to individual response. Start with 10 mg 4 times daily for the first 2 to 4 days, increase to 25 mg 4 times daily for balance of first week. For second and subsequent weeks, increase dosage to 50 mg 4 times daily. For maintenance, adjust dosage to lowest effective levels.

The incidence of toxic reactions, particularly the L. E. cell syndrome, is high in the group of patients receiving large doses of Apresoline.

In a few resistant patients, up to 300 mg Apresoline daily may be required for a significant

Apresoline® hydrochloride (hydralazine hydrochloride USP)

antihypertensive effect. In such cases, a lower dosage of Apresoline combined with a thiazide, reserpine, or both may be considered. However, when combining therapy, individual titration is essential to insure the lowest possible therapeutic dose of each drug.

HOW SUPPLIED

Tablets, 10 mg (pale yellow, dry-coated); bottles of 100 and 1000.

Tablets, 25 mg (deep blue, dry-coated) and 50 mg (light blue, dry-coated); bottles of 100, 500, 1000 and Accu-Pak® blister units of 100.

Tablets, 100 mg (peach, dry-coated); bottles of 100.

Dispense in tight, light-resistant container (USP).

C80-15 (1/80)

Ismelin® sulfate
(guanethidine monosulfate)

INDICATIONS

Moderate and severe hypertension either alone or as an adjunct.

Renal hypertension, including that secondary to pyelonephritis, renal amyloidosis, and renal artery stenosis.

CONTRAINDICATIONS

Known or suspected pheochromocytoma; hypersensitivity; frank congestive heart failure not due to hypertension; use of MAO inhibitors.

WARNINGS

Ismelin is a potent drug and can lead to disturbing and serious clinical problems. Before prescribing, physicians should familiarize themselves with the details of its use and warn patients not to deviate from instructions.

> Orthostatic hypotension can occur frequently and patients should be properly instructed about this potential hazard. Fainting spells may occur unless the patient is forewarned to sit or lie down with the onset of dizziness or weakness. Postural hypotension is most marked in the morning and is accentuated by hot weather, alcohol, or exercise. Dizziness or weakness may be particularly bothersome during the initial period of dosage adjustment and with postural changes, such as arising in the morning. The potential occurrence of these symptoms may require alteration of previous daily activity. The patient should be cautioned to avoid sudden or prolonged standing or exercise while taking the drug.

Concurrent use of Ismelin and rauwolfia derivatives may cause excessive postural hypotension, bradycardia, and mental depression.

If possible, withdraw therapy two weeks prior to surgery to reduce the possibility of vascular collapse and cardiac arrest during anesthesia. If emergency surgery is indicated, preanesthetic and anesthetic agents should be administered cautiously in reduced dosage. Oxygen, atropine, vasopressors, and adequate solutions for volume replacement should be ready for immediate use to counteract vascular collapse in the surgical patient. Vasopressors should be used only with extreme caution, since Ismelin augments the responsiveness to exogenously administered norepinephrine and vasopressors with respect to blood pressure and their propensity for the production of cardiac arrhythmias.

Dosage requirements may be reduced in the presence of fever.

Exercise special care when treating patients with a history of bronchial asthma; asthmatics are more apt to be hypersensitive to catecholamine depletion and their condition may be aggravated.

Usage in Pregnancy

The safety of Ismelin for use in pregnancy has not been established; therefore this drug should be used in pregnant patients only when, in the judgment of the physician, its use is deemed essential to the welfare of the patient.

PRECAUTIONS

The effects of guanethidine are cumulative over long periods; initial doses should be small and increased gradually in small increments.

Use very cautiously in hypertensive patients with: renal disease and nitrogen retention or rising BUN levels, since decreased blood pressure may further compromise renal function; coronary disease with insufficiency or recent myocardial infarction; cerebral vascular disease, especially with encephalopathy.

Do not give to patients with severe cardiac failure except with extreme caution since Ismelin may interfere with the compensatory role of the adrenergic system in producing circulatory adjustment in patients with congestive heart failure.

In patients with incipient cardiac decompensation, watch for weight gain or edema, which may be averted by the concomitant administration of a thiazide.

Remember that both digitalis and Ismelin slow the heart rate.

Use cautiously in patients with a history of peptic ulcer or other chronic disorders which may be aggravated by a relative increase in parasympathetic tone.

Amphetamine-like compounds, stimulants (*eg,* ephedrine, methylphenidate), tricyclic antidepressants (*eg,* amitriptyline, imipramine, desipramine) and other psychopharmacologic agents (*eg,* phenothiazines and related compounds), and oral contraceptives may reduce the hypotensive effect of guanethidine.

MAO inhibitors should be discontinued for at least one week before starting therapy with Ismelin.

ADVERSE REACTIONS

Frequent reactions due to sympathetic blockade: dizziness, weakness, lassitude, and syncope resulting from either postural or exertional hypotension.

Frequent reactions due to unopposed parasympathetic activity: bradycardia, increase in bowel movements, and diarrhea. Diarrhea may be severe at times and necessitate discontinuation of the medication.

Other common reactions: inhibition of ejaculation, a tendency toward fluid retention and edema with occasional development of congestive heart failure.

Other less common reactions: dyspnea, fatigue, nausea, vomiting, nocturia, urinary incontinence, dermatitis, scalp hair loss, dry mouth, rise in BUN, ptosis of the lids, blurring of vision, parotid tenderness, myalgia, muscle tremor, mental depression, chest pains (angina), chest paresthesias, nasal congestion, weight gain, and asthma in susceptible individuals. Although a causal relationship has not been established, a few instances of blood dyscrasias (anemia, thrombocytopenia, and leukopenia) and of priapism have been reported.

DOSAGE AND ADMINISTRATION

Better control may be obtained, especially in the initial phases of treatment, if the patient can have his blood pressure recorded regularly at home.

Ambulatory Patients. Begin treatment with small doses (10 mg). Increase gradually, depending upon the patient's response. Ismelin has a long duration of action; therefore, dosage increases should not be made more often than every 5 to 7 days, unless the patient is hospitalized.

Take blood pressure in the supine position, after standing for ten minutes, and immediately after exercise if feasible. Increase dosage only if there has been *no* decrease in standing blood pressure from the previous levels. The average daily dose is 25 to 50 mg; only 1 dose a day is usually required.

Ismelin® sulfate (guanethidine monosulfate)

Dosage Chart for Ambulatory Patients

Visits at Intervals of 5 to 7 Days   *Daily Dose*
Visit No. 1 (Start with 10-mg tablets) . . . . 10 mg
Visit No. 2 . . . . 20 mg
Visit No. 3 (Patient can be changed to 25-mg tablets
     whenever convenient) . . . . 30 mg
                         (three 10-mg tablets)
                              or 37.5 mg
            (one and one-half 25-mg tablets)
Visit No. 4 . . . . 50 mg
Visit No. 5 (and subsequent). Dosage may be increased by
12.5 mg or 25 mg if necessary.

     Reduce dosage in any of the following 3 situations:
       1. *Normal supine pressure*
       2. *Excessive orthostatic fall in pressure*
       3. *Severe diarrhea*

Hospitalized Patients. Initial oral dose is 25 to 50 mg, increased by 25 or 50 mg daily or every other day as indicated. This higher dosage is possible because hospitalized patients can be watched carefully. Unless absolutely impossible, take the standing blood pressure regularly. Patients should not be discharged from the hospital until the effect of the drug on the standing blood pressure is known. *Patients should be told about the possibility of orthostatic hypotension and warned not to get out of bed without help during the period of dosage adjustment.*

Combination Therapy. Ismelin may be added gradually to thiazides and/or hydralazine. Thiazide diuretics enhance the effectiveness of Ismelin and may reduce the incidence of edema. When thiazide diuretics are added to the regimen in patients on Ismelin, it is usually necessary to reduce the dosage of Ismelin. After control is established, reduce dosage of all drugs to the lowest effective level.
     When replacing MAO inhibitors, at least one week should elapse before commencing treatment with Ismelin.
     In many cases ganglionic blockers will have been stopped before Ismelin is started. It may be advisable, however, to withdraw the blocker gradually to prevent a spiking blood pressure response during the transfer period.

OVERDOSAGE

Signs and Symptoms

Postural hypotension [with dizziness, blurring of vision, etc., possibly progressing to syncope when standing] and bradycardia are most likely to occur; diarrhea, possibly severe, also may occur. Unconsciousness is unlikely if adequate blood pressure and cerebral perfusion can be maintained by appropriate positioning [supine] and by other treatment as required.

Treatment

In previously normotensive patients, treatment has consisted essentially of restoring blood pressure and heart rate to normal by keeping patient in supine position. Normal homeostatic control usually returns gradually over a 72-hour period in these patients.
     In previously hypertensive patients, particularly those with impaired cardiac reserve or other cardiovascular-renal disease, intensive treatment may be required to support vital functions and/or to control cardiac irregularities that might be present. Supine position must be maintained; if vasopressors are required, it must be remembered that Ismelin may increase responsiveness as to blood pressure rise and occurrence of cardiac arrhythmias.
     Diarrhea, if severe or persistent, should be treated symptomatically to reduce intestinal hypermotility, with due attention to maintenance of hydration and electrolyte balance.

HOW SUPPLIED

Tablets 10 mg — pale yellow, scored (imprinted 49 CIBA)
     Bottles of 100 . . . . NDC 0083-0049-30
     Bottles of 1000 . . . . NDC 0083-0049-40

Consumer Pack — One Unit
     (12 bottles-100 tablets each) . . . . NDC 0083-0049-65

Accu-Pak® Unit Dose (blister pack)
     Box of 100 (strips of 10) . . . . NDC 0083-0049-32

Tablets 25 mg — white, scored (imprinted 103 CIBA)
     Bottles of 100 . . . . NDC 0083-0103-30
     Bottles of 1000 . . . . NDC 0083-0103-40
Consumer Pack — One Unit
     (12 bottles-100 tablets each) . . . . NDC 0083-0103-65
Accu-Pak® Unit Dose (blister pack)
     Box of 100 (strips of 10) . . . . NDC 0083-0103-32

Dispense in tight container (USP).

C81-20 (6/81)

Lithobid®
lithium carbonate
slow-release tablets
(not USP)

Cibalith-S™ Syrup
lithium citrate

> **WARNING**
>
> Lithium toxicity is closely related to serum lithium levels, and can occur at doses close to therapeutic levels. Facilities for prompt and accurate serum lithium determinations should be available before initiating therapy.

INDICATIONS

Lithium is indicated in the treatment of manic episodes of manic-depressive illness. Maintenance therapy prevents or diminishes the intensity of subsequent episodes in those manic-depressive patients with a history of mania.

<u>Typical symptoms</u> of mania include pressure of speech, motor hyperactivity, reduced need for sleep, flight of ideas, grandiosity, elation, poor judgment, aggressiveness, and possibly hostility. When given to a patient experiencing a manic episode, lithium may produce a normalization of symptomatology within 1 to 3 weeks.

WARNINGS

Lithium should generally not be given to patients with significant renal or cardiovascular disease, severe debilitation or dehydration, or sodium depletion, and to patients receiving diuretics, since the risk of lithium toxicity is very high in such patients. If the psychiatric indication is life-threatening, and if such a patient fails to respond to other measures, lithium treatment may be undertaken with extreme caution, including daily serum lithium determinations and adjustment to the usually low doses ordinarily tolerated by these individuals. In such instances, hospitalization is a necessity.

Lithium toxicity is closely related to serum lithium levels, and can occur at doses close to therapeutic levels (see **DOSAGE AND ADMINISTRATION**).

Lithium therapy has been reported in some cases to be associated with morphologic changes in the kidneys. The relationship between such changes and renal function has not been established.

Outpatients and their families should be warned that the patient must discontinue lithium therapy and contact his physician if such clinical signs of lithium toxicity as diarrhea, vomiting, tremor, mild ataxia, drowsiness, or muscular weakness occur.

Lithium may prolong the effects of neuromuscular blocking agents. Therefore, neuromuscular blocking agents should be given with caution to patients receiving lithium.

Lithium may impair mental and/or physical abilities. Caution patients about activities requiring alertness (e.g., operating vehicles or machinery).

<u>Combined use of haloperidol and lithium</u>: An encephalopathic syndrome (characterized by weakness, lethargy, fever, tremulousness and confusion, extrapyramidal symp-

Lithobid® lithium carbonate tablets
Cibalith-S™ lithium citrate syrup.

toms, leucocytosis, elevated serum enzymes, BUN and FBS) followed by irreversible brain damage has occurred in a few patients treated with lithium plus haloperidol. A causal relationship between these events and the concomitant administration of lithium and haloperidol has not been established; however, patients receiving such combined therapy should be monitored closely for early evidence of neurological toxicity and treatment discontinued promptly if such signs appear. The possibility of similar adverse interactions with other antipsychotic medications exists.

Usage in Pregnancy: Adverse effects on nidation in rats, embryo viability in mice, and metabolism in vitro of rat testis and human spermatozoa have been attributed to lithium, as have teratogenicity in submammalian species and cleft palates in mice. Studies in rats, rabbits and monkeys have shown no evidence of lithium-induced teratology.
There are lithium birth registries in the United States and elsewhere; however there are at the present time insufficient data to determine the effects of lithium on human fetuses. Therefore, at this point, lithium should not be used in pregnancy, especially the first trimester, unless in the opinion of the physician, the potential benefits outweigh the possible hazards.

Usage in Nursing Mothers: Lithium is excreted in human milk. Nursing should not be undertaken during lithium therapy except in rare and unusual circumstances where, in the view of the physician, the potential benefits to the mother outweigh possible hazards to the child.

Usage in Children: Since information regarding the safety and effectiveness of lithium in children under 12 years of age is not available, its use in such patients is not recommended at this time.

PRECAUTIONS
The ability to tolerate lithium is greater during the acute manic phase and decreases when manic symptoms subside (see **DOSAGE AND ADMINISTRATION**).

The distribution space of lithium approximates that of total body water. Lithium is primarily excreted in urine with insignificant excretion in feces. Renal excretion of lithium is proportional to its plasma concentration. The half-elimination time of lithium is approximately 24 hours. Lithium decreases sodium reabsorption by the renal tubules which could lead to sodium depletion. Therefore, it is essential for the patient to maintain a normal diet, including salt, and an adequate fluid intake (2500-3000 ml) at least during the initial stabilization period. Decreased tolerance to lithium has been reported to ensue from protracted sweating or diarrhea and, if such occur, supplemental fluid and salt should be administered.

In addition to sweating and diarrhea, concomitant infection with elevated temperatures may also necessitate a temporary reduction or cessation of medication.

Previously existing underlying disorders do not necessarily constitute a contraindication to lithium treatment; where hypothyroidism exists, careful monitoring of thyroid function during lithium stabilization and maintenance allows for correction of changing thyroid parameters, if any, where hypothyroidism occurs during lithium stabilization and maintenance, supplemental thyroid treatment may be used.

Indomethacin (50 mg t.i.d.) has been reported to increase steady-state plasma lithium levels from 30 to 59 percent. There is also some evidence that other nonsteroidal, anti-inflammatory agents may have a similar effect. When such combinations are used, increased plasma lithium level monitoring is recommended.

ADVERSE REACTIONS
Adverse reactions are seldom encountered at serum lithium levels below 1.5 mEq/l, except in the occasional patient sensitive to lithium. Mild-to-moderate toxic reactions may occur at levels from 1.5-2.5 mEq/l, and moderate-to-severe reactions may be seen at levels from 2.0-2.5 mEq/l, depending upon individual response to the drug.

Fine hand tremor, polyuria and mild thirst may occur during initial therapy for the acute manic phase, and may persist throughout treatment. Transient and mild nausea and general discomfort may also appear during the first few days of lithium administration.

These side effects are an inconvenience rather than a disabling condition, and usually subside with continued treatment or a temporary reduction or cessation of dosage. If persistent, a cessation of dosage is indicated.

Diarrhea, vomiting, drowsiness, muscular weakness and lack of coordination may be early signs of lithium intoxication, and can occur at lithium levels below 2.0 mEq/l. At higher levels, giddiness, ataxia, blurred vision, tinnitus and a large output of dilute urine may be seen. Serum lithium levels above 3.0 mEq/l may produce a complex clinical picture involving multiple organs and organ systems. Serum lithium levels should not be permitted to exceed 2.0 mEq/l during the acute treatment phase.

The following toxic reactions have been reported and appear to be related to serum lithium levels, including levels within the therapeutic range.

Neuromuscular: tremor, muscle hyperirritability (fasciculations, twitching, clonic movements of whole limbs), ataxia, choreoathetotic movements, hyperactive deep tendon reflexes.

Central Nervous System: blackout spells, epileptiform seizures, slurred speech, dizziness, vertigo, incontinence of urine or feces, somnolence, psychomotor retardation, restlessness, confusion, stupor, coma.

Cardiovascular: cardiac arrhythmia, hypotension, peripheral circulatory collapse.

Gastrointestinal: anorexia, nausea, vomiting, diarrhea.

Genitourinary: albuminuria, oliguria, polyuria, glycosuria.

Dermatologic: drying and thinning of hair, anesthesia of skin, chronic folliculitis, xerosis cutis, alopecia, exacerbation of psoriasis.

Autonomic Nervous System: blurred vision, dry mouth.

Miscellaneous: fatigue, lethargy, tendency to sleep, dehydration, weight loss, transient scotomata.

Thyroid Abnormalities: euthyroid goiter and/or hypothyroidism (including myxedema) accompanied by lower T_3 and T_4, I_{131} iodine uptake may be elevated (see **PRECAUTIONS**). Paradoxically, rare cases of hyperthyroidism have been reported.

EEG Changes: diffuse slowing, widening of frequency spectrum, potentiation and disorganization of background rhythm.

EKG Changes: reversible flattening, isoelectricity or inversion of T-waves.

Miscellaneous reactions unrelated to dosage are: transient electroencephalographic and electrocardiographic changes, leucocytosis, headache, diffuse nontoxic goiter with or without hypothyroidism, transient hyperglycemia, generalized pruritus with or without rash, cutaneous ulcers, albuminuria, worsening of organic brain syndromes, excessive weight gain, edematous swelling of ankles or wrists, and thirst or polyuria, sometimes resembling diabetes insipidus and metallic taste.

A single report has been received of the development of painful discoloration of fingers and toes and coldness of the extremities within one day of the starting of treatment of lithium. The mechanism through which these symptoms (resembling Raynaud's Syndrome) developed is not known. Recovery followed discontinuance.

DOSAGE AND ADMINISTRATION
Acute Mania: Optimal patient response can usually be established and maintained with the following dosages:

Lithobid .... 900 mg b.i.d. or 600 mg t.i.d. (1800 mg per day)
Cibalith-S .... 10 ml (2 teaspoons) (16 mEq of lithium) t.i.d.

Such doses will normally produce an effective serum lithium level ranging between 1.0 and 1.5 mEq/l. Dosage

Lithobid® lithium carbonate tablets
Cibalith-S™ lithium citrate syrup.

must be individualized according to serum levels and clinical response. Regular monitoring of the patient's clinical state and of serum lithium levels is necessary. Serum levels should be determined twice per week during the acute phase, and until the serum level and clinical condition of the patient have been stabilized.

Long-Term Control: The desirable serum lithium levels are 0.6 to 1.2 mEq/l. Dosage will vary from one individual to another, but usually the following dosages will maintain this level:

Lithobid   . . . . .900 mg to 1200 mg per day given in
two or three divided doses.
Cibalith-S   . . . . .5 ml (1 teaspoon) (8 mEq of lithium)
t.i.d. or q.i.d.

Serum lithium levels in uncomplicated cases receiving maintenance therapy during remission should be monitored at least every two months. Patients abnormally sensitive to lithium may exhibit toxic signs at serum levels of 1.0 to 1.5 mEq/l. Elderly patients often respond to reduced dosage, and may exhibit signs of toxicity at serum levels ordinarily tolerated by other patients.

N.B.: Blood samples for serum lithium determinations should be drawn immediately prior to the next dose when lithium concentrations are relatively stable (i.e., 8-12 hours after previous dose). Total reliance must not be placed on serum levels alone. Accurate patient evaluation requires both clinical and laboratory analysis.

OVERDOSAGE
The toxic levels for lithium are close to the therapeutic levels. It is therefore important that patients and their families be cautioned to watch for early toxic symptoms and to discontinue the drug and inform the physician should they occur. Toxic symptoms are listed in detail under **ADVERSE REACTIONS.**

Treatment: No specific antidote for lithium poisoning is known. Early symptoms of lithium toxicity can usually be treated by reduction or cessation of dosage of the drug and resumption of the treatment at a lower dose after 24 to 48 hours. In severe cases of lithium poisoning, the first and foremost goal of treatment consists of elimination of this ion from the patient.

Treatment is essentially the same as that used in barbiturate poisoning: 1) gastric lavage 2) correction of fluid and electrolyte imbalance and 3) regulation of kidney functioning. Urea, mannitol, and aminophylline all produce significant increases in lithium excretion. Hemodialysis is an effective and rapid means of removing the ion from the severely toxic patient. Infection prophylaxis, regular chest x-rays, and preservation of adequate respiration are essential.

HOW SUPPLIED
Lithobid, lithium carbonate 300 mg, peach-colored, slow-release tablets are supplied in bottles of 100's & 1000's and in unit-dose boxes of 100's.

Cibalith-S, lithium citrate syrup, 8 mEq of lithium ion per 5 ml (1 teaspoon) is supplied as a sugar-free, raspberry-flavored syrup in bottles of 480 ml.

C81-70 (1/82)

Ludiomil®
maprotiline hydrochloride   **Tablets**

INDICATIONS AND USAGE

Ludiomil is indicated for the treatment of depressive illness in patients with depressive neurosis (dysthymic disorder) and manic-depressive illness, depressed type (major depressive disorder). Ludiomil is also effective for the relief of anxiety associated with depression.

CONTRAINDICATIONS
Ludiomil is contraindicated in patients hypersensitive to Ludiomil and in patients with known or suspected seizure disorders. It should not be given concomitantly with monoamine oxidase (MAO) inhibitors. A minimum of 14 days should be allowed to elapse after discontinuation of MAO inhibitors before treatment with Ludiomil is initiated. Effects should be monitored with gradual increase in dosage until optimum response is achieved. The drug is not recommended for use during the acute phase of myocardial infarction.

WARNINGS
Extreme caution should be used when this drug is given to:
—patients with a history of myocardial infarction;
—patients with a history or presence of cardiovascular disease because of the possibility of conduction defects, arrhythmias, myocardial infarction, strokes and tachycardia.

PRECAUTIONS
General: The possibility of suicide in seriously depressed patients is inherent in their illness and may persist until significant remission occurs. Therefore, patients must be carefully supervised during all phases of treatment with Ludiomil, and prescriptions should be written for the smallest number of tablets consistent with good patient management.

Seizures have been reported in patients treated with Ludiomil. These have occurred in patients both with and without a past history of seizures. While it must be noted that a cause-and-effect relationship has not been established, the risk of seizures may be reduced by initiating therapy at low dosage. Because of the long half-life of Ludiomil (average 51 hours) initial dosage should be maintained for two weeks before being raised gradually in small increments (see **DOSAGE AND ADMINISTRATION**).

Hypomanic or manic episodes have been known to occur in some patients taking tricyclic antidepressant drugs, particularly in patients with cyclic disorders. Such occurrences have also been noted, rarely, with Ludiomil.

Prior to elective surgery, Ludiomil should be discontinued for as long as clinically feasible, since little is known about the interaction between Ludiomil and general anesthetics.

Ludiomil should be administered with caution in patients with increased intraocular pressure, history of urinary retention, or history of narrow-angle glaucoma because of the drug's anticholinergic properties.
Information for Patients: Warn patients to exercise caution about potentially hazardous tasks, or operating automobiles or machinery since the drug may impair mental and/or physical abilities.

Ludiomil may enhance the response to alcohol, barbiturates, and other CNS depressants, requiring appropriate caution of administration.
Laboratory Tests: Although not observed with Ludiomil, the drug should be discontinued if there is evidence of pathologic neutrophil depression. Leukocyte and differential counts should be performed in patients who develop fever and sore throat during therapy.
Drug Interactions: Close supervision and careful adjustment of dosage are required when administering Ludiomil concomitantly with anti-

Ludiomil® maprotiline hydrochloride

cholinergic or sympathomimetic drugs because of the possibility of additive atropine-like effects.

Concurrent administration of Ludiomil with electroshock therapy should be avoided because of the lack of experience in this area.

Caution should be exercised when administering Ludiomil to hyperthyroid patients or those on thyroid medication because of the possibility of enhanced potential for cardiovascular toxicity of Ludiomil.

Ludiomil should be used with caution in patients receiving guanethidine or similar agents since it may block the pharmacologic effects of these drugs.

(See **Information for Patients**.)

Carcinogenesis, Mutagenesis, Impairment of Fertility: Carcinogenicity and chronic toxicity studies have been conducted in laboratory rats and dogs. No drug- or dose-related occurrence of carcinogenesis was evident in rats receiving daily oral doses up to 60 mg/kg of Ludiomil for eighteen months or in dogs receiving daily oral doses up to 30 mg/kg of Ludiomil for one year. In addition, no evidence of mutagenic activity was found in offspring of female mice mated with males treated with up to 60 times the maximum daily human dose.

Pregnancy Category B: Reproduction studies have been performed in female laboratory rabbits, mice, and rats at doses up to 1.3, 7, and 9 times the maximum daily human dose respectively and have revealed no evidence of impaired fertility or harm to the fetus due to Ludiomil. There are, however, no adequate and well-controlled studies in pregnant women. Because animal reproduction studies are not always predictive of human response, this drug should be used during pregnancy only if clearly needed.

Labor and Delivery: Although the effect of Ludiomil on labor and delivery is unknown, caution should be exercised as with any drug with CNS depressant action.

Nursing Mothers: Ludiomil is excreted in breast milk. At steady state, the concentrations in milk correspond closely to the concentrations in whole blood. Caution should be exercised when Ludiomil is administered to a nursing woman.

Pediatric Use: Safety and effectiveness in children below the age of 18 have not been established.

ADVERSE REACTIONS

The following adverse reactions have been noted with Ludiomil and are generally similar to those observed with tricyclic antidepressants.

Cardiovascular: Rare occurrences of hypotension, hypertension, tachycardia, palpitation, arrhythmia, heart block, and syncope have been reported with Ludiomil.

Psychiatric: Nervousness (6%), anxiety (3%), insomnia (2%), and agitation (2%); rarely, confusional states (especially in the elderly), hallucinations, disorientation, delusions, restlessness, nightmares, hypomania, mania, exacerbation of psychosis, decrease in memory, and feelings of unreality.

Neurological: Drowsiness (16%), dizziness (8%), tremor (3%), and, rarely, numbness, tingling, motor hyperactivity, akathisia, seizures, EEG alterations, tinnitus, extrapyramidal symptoms, ataxia, and dysarthria.

Anticholinergic: Dry mouth (22%), constipation (6%), and blurred vision (4%); rarely, accommodation disturbances, mydriasis, urinary retention, and delayed micturition.

Allergic: Rare instances of skin rash, petechiae, itching, photosensitization, edema, and drug fever.

Gastrointestinal: Nausea (2%) and, rarely, vomiting, epigastric distress, diarrhea, bitter taste, abdominal cramps and dysphagia.

Endocrine: Rare instances of increased or decreased libido, impotence, and elevation or depression of blood sugar levels.

Other: Weakness and fatigue (4%) and headache (4%); rarely, altered liver function, jaundice, weight loss or gain, excessive perspiration, flushing, urinary frequency, increased salivation, and nasal congestion.

Note: Although the following adverse reactions have not been reported with Ludiomil, its pharmacologic similarity to tricyclic antidepressants requires that each reaction be considered when administering Ludiomil.

—Bone marrow depression, including agranulocytosis, eosinophilia, purpura, and thrombocytopenia, myocardial infarction, stroke, peripheral neuropathy, sublingual adenitis, black tongue, stomatitis, paralytic ileus, gynecomastia in the male, breast enlargement and galactorrhea in the female, and testicular swelling.

OVERDOSAGE

Animal Oral LD$_{50}$: The oral LD$_{50}$ of Ludiomil is 600-750 mg/kg in mice, 760-900 mg/kg in rats, > 1000 mg/kg in rabbits, > 300 mg/kg in cats, and > 30 mg/kg in dogs.

Signs and Symptoms: Data dealing with overdosage in humans are limited with only a few cases on record. Symptoms are drowsiness, tachycardia, ataxia, vomiting, cyanosis, hypotension, shock, restlessness, agitation, hyperpyrexia, muscle rigidity, athetoid movements, mydriasis, cardiac arrhythmias, impaired cardiac condition. In severe cases, loss of consciousness and generalized convulsions may occur. Since congestive heart failure has been seen with overdosages of tricyclic antidepressants, it should be considered with Ludiomil overdosage.

Treatment: There is no specific antidote. Induced emesis and gastric lavage are recommended. It may be helpful to leave the tube in the stomach with irrigation and continual aspiration of stomach contents possibly promoting more rapid elimination of the drug from the body. The room should be darkened, allowing only minimal external stimulation to reduce the tendency to convulsions.

1. The intravenous administration of 1 to 3 mg of physostigmine has been reported to reverse the signs and symptoms of overdosage with tricyclic antidepressants. Repeat doses at intervals of 30 to 60 minutes may be necessary.

2. Hyperirritability and convulsions may be treated with carefully titrated parenteral barbiturates. Barbiturates should not be employed, however, if drugs that inhibit monoamine oxidase have also been taken by the patient in overdosage or in recent therapy. Similarly, barbiturates may induce respiratory depression, particularly in children. It is therefore advisable to have equipment available for artificial ventilation and resuscitation when barbiturates are employed. Paraldehyde may be used effectively in some children to counteract muscular hypertonus and convulsions with less likelihood of causing respiratory depression.

Ludiomil® maprotiline hydrochloride

3. Shock (circulatory collapse) should be treated with supportive measures such as intravenous fluids, oxygen, and corticosteroids.
4. Hyperpyrexia should be controlled by whatever means available, including ice packs if necessary.
5. Signs of congestive heart failure may be satisfactorily treated by rapid digitalization.
6. Dialysis is of little value because of the low plasma concentration of this drug.

DOSAGE AND ADMINISTRATION

A single daily dose is an alternative to divided daily doses. Therapeutic effects are sometimes seen within 3 to 7 days, although as long as 2 to 3 weeks are usually necessary.

Initial Adult Dosage: An initial dosage of 75 mg daily is suggested for outpatients with mild-to-moderate depression. However, in some patients, particularly the elderly, an initial dosage of 25 mg daily may be used. Because of the long half-life of Ludiomil, the initial dosage should be maintained for two weeks. The dosage may then be increased gradually in 25 mg increments as required and tolerated. Most patients respond to a dose of 150 mg daily, but daily dosage as high as 225 mg may be required in some cases.

More severely depressed, hospitalized patients should be given an initial daily dose of 100 mg to 150 mg which may be gradually increased as required and tolerated. Most hospitalized patients with moderate-to-severe depression respond to a daily dosage of 150 mg to 225 mg, although dosages as high as 300 mg may be required in some cases. Daily dosage of 300 mg should not be exceeded.

Elderly Patients: In general, lower dosages are recommended for patients over 60 years of age. Dosages of 50 mg to 75 mg daily are usually satisfactory as maintenance therapy for elderly patients who do not tolerate higher amounts.

Maintenance: Dosage during prolonged maintenance therapy should be kept at the lowest effective level. Dosage may be reduced to levels of 75 mg to 150 mg daily during such periods, with subsequent adjustment depending on therapeutic response.

HOW SUPPLIED

Tablets 25 mg—oval, dark orange, coated (imprinted CIBA 110)
　　Bottle of 100 — NDC 0083-0110-30
　　Accu-Pak® Unit Dose (blister pack)
　　　　Box of 100 (strips of 10) — NDC 0083-0110-32
Tablets 50 mg—round, dark orange, coated imprinted CIBA 26)
　　Bottle of 100 — NDC 0083-0026-30
　　Accu-Pak® Unit Dose (blister pack)
　　　　Box of 100 (strips of 10) — NDC 0083-0026-32
Tablets 75 mg—oval, white, coated (imprinted 135 CIBA)
　　Bottle of 100 — NDC 0083-0135-30
　　Accu-Pak® Unit Dose (blister pack)
　　　　Box of 100 (strips of 10) — NDC 0083-0135-32

Dispense in tight container (USP).

1. Alkalay D, et al. Bioavailability and kinetics of maprotiline. *Clin Pharmacol Ther* 1980; **27** (5): 697-703.
2. Riess W, et al. The pharmacokinetic properties of maprotiline (Ludiomil®) in man. *J Int Med Res* 1975; **3** (2): 16-41.　　C82-57 (Rev.10/82)

Ritalin® hydrochloride (methylphenidate hydrochloride USP) Tablets

Ritalin-SR® (methylphenidate hydrochloride) sustained-release tablets

INDICATIONS

Based on a review of this drug by the National Academy of Sciences-National Research Council and/or other information, FDA has classified the indications as follows:

Effective: Attention Deficit Disorders (previously known as Minimal Brain Dysfunction in Children). Other terms being used to describe the behavioral syndrome below include: Hyperkinetic Child Syndrome, Minimal Brain Damage, Minimal Cerebral Dysfunction, Minor Cerebral Dysfunction.

Ritalin is indicated as an integral part of a total treatment program which typically includes other remedial measures (psychological, educational, social) for a stabilizing effect in children with a behavioral syndrome characterized by the following group of developmentally inappropriate symptoms: moderate-to-severe distractibility, short attention span, hyperactivity, emotional lability, and impulsivity. The diagnosis of this syndrome should not be made with finality when these symptoms are only of comparatively recent origin. Nonlocalizing (soft) neurological signs, learning disability, and abnormal EEG may or may not be present, and a diagnosis of central nervous system dysfunction may or may not be warranted.

Special Diagnostic Considerations

Specific etiology of this syndrome is unknown, and there is no single diagnostic test. Adequate diagnosis requires the use not only of medical but of special psychological, educational, and social resources.

Characteristics commonly reported include: chronic history of short attention span, distractibility, emotional lability, impulsivity, and moderate-to-severe hyperactivity; minor neurological signs and abnormal EEG. Learning may or may not be impaired. The diagnosis must be based upon a complete history and evaluation of the child and not solely on the presence of one or more of these characteristics.

Drug treatment is not indicated for all children with this syndrome. Stimulants are not intended for use in the child who exhibits symptoms secondary to environmental factors and/or primary psychiatric disorders, including psychosis. Appropriate educational placement is essential and psychosocial intervention is generally necessary. When remedial measures alone are insufficient, the decision to prescribe stimulant medication will depend upon the physician's assessment of the chronicity and severity of the child's symptoms.

Effective: Narcolepsy

"Possibly" effective: Mild depression; Apathetic or Withdrawn Senile Behavior

Final classification of the less-than-effective indications requires further investigation.

CONTRAINDICATIONS

Marked anxiety, tension, and agitation are contraindications to Ritalin, since the drug may aggravate these symptoms. Ritalin is contraindicated also in patients known to be hypersensitive to the drug, in patients with

Ritalin® hydrochloride (methylphenidate hydrochloride USP)
Ritalin-SR® (methylphenidate hydrochloride)

glaucoma, and in patients with motor tics or with a family history or diagnosis of Tourette's syndrome.

WARNINGS

Ritalin should not be used in children under six years, since safety and efficacy in this age group have not been established.

Sufficient data on safety and efficacy of long-term use of Ritalin in children are not yet available. Although a causal relationship has not been established, suppression of growth (ie, weight gain, and/or height) has been reported with the long-term use of stimulants in children. Therefore, patients requiring long-term therapy should be carefully monitored.

Ritalin should not be used for severe depression of either exogenous or endogenous origin. Clinical experience suggests that in psychotic children, administration of Ritalin may exacerbate symptoms of behavior disturbance and thought disorder.

Ritalin should not be used for the prevention or treatment of normal fatigue states.

There is some clinical evidence that Ritalin may lower the convulsive threshold in patients with prior history of seizures, with prior EEG abnormalities in absence of seizures, and, very rarely, in absence of history of seizures and no prior EEG evidence of seizures. Safe concomitant use of anticonvulsants and Ritalin has not been established. In the presence of seizures, the drug should be discontinued.

Use cautiously in patients with hypertension. Blood pressure should be monitored at appropriate intervals in all patients taking Ritalin, especially those with hypertension.

Symptoms of visual disturbances have been encountered in rare cases. Difficulties with accommodation and blurring of vision have been reported.

Drug Interactions

Ritalin may decrease the hypotensive effect of guanethidine. Use cautiously with pressor agents and MAO inhibitors.

Human pharmacologic studies have shown that Ritalin may inhibit the metabolism of coumarin anticoagulants, anticonvulsants (phenobarbital, diphenylhydantoin, primidone), phenylbutazone, and tricyclic antidepressants (imipramine, desipramine). Downward dosage adjustments of these drugs may be required when given concomitantly with Ritalin.

Usage in Pregnancy

Adequate animal reproduction studies to establish safe use of Ritalin during pregnancy have not been conducted. Therefore, until more information is available, Ritalin should not be prescribed for women of childbearing age unless, in the opinion of the physician, the potential benefits outweigh the possible risks.

Drug Dependence

Ritalin should be given cautiously to emotionally unstable patients, such as those with a history of drug dependence or alcoholism, because such patients may increase dosage on their own initiative.

Chronically abusive use can lead to marked tolerance and psychic dependence with varying degrees of abnormal behavior. Frank psychotic episodes can occur, especially with parenteral abuse. Careful supervision is required during drug withdrawal, since severe depression as well as the effects of chronic overactivity can be unmasked. Long-term follow-up may be required because of the patient's basic personality disturbances.

PRECAUTIONS

Patients with an element of agitation may react ad-

versely; discontinue therapy if necessary.

Periodic CBC, differential, and platelet counts are advised during prolonged therapy.

Drug treatment is not indicated in all cases of this behavioral syndrome and should be considered only in light of the complete history and evaluation of the child. The decision to prescribe Ritalin should depend on the physician's assessment of the chronicity and severity of the child's symptoms and their appropriateness for his/her age. Prescription should not depend solely on the presence of one or more of the behavioral characteristics.

When these symptoms are associated with acute stress reactions, treatment with Ritalin is usually not indicated.

Long-term effects of Ritalin in children have not been well established.

ADVERSE REACTIONS

Nervousness and insomnia are the most common adverse reactions but are usually controlled by reducing dosage and omitting the drug in the afternoon or evening. Other reactions include hypersensitivity (including skin rash, urticaria, fever, arthralgia, exfoliative dermatitis, erythema multiforme with histopathological findings of necrotizing vasculitis, and thrombocytopenic purpura); anorexia; nausea; dizziness; palpitations; headache; dyskinesia; drowsiness; blood pressure and pulse changes, both up and down; tachycardia; angina; cardiac arrhythmia; abdominal pain; weight loss during prolonged therapy. There have been rare reports of Tourette's syndrome. Toxic psychosis has been reported. Although a definite causal relationship has not been established, the following have been reported in patients taking this drug: leukopenia and/or anemia; a few instances of scalp hair loss.

In children, loss of appetite, abdominal pain, weight loss during prolonged therapy, insomnia, and tachycardia may occur more frequently; however, any of the other adverse reactions listed above may also occur.

DOSAGE AND ADMINISTRATION

Dosage should be individualized according to the needs and responses of the patient.

Adults

Tablets: Administer in divided doses 2 or 3 times daily, preferably 30-45 minutes before meals. Average dosage is 20 to 30 mg daily. Some patients may require 40 to 60 mg daily. In others, 10 to 15 mg daily will be adequate. Patients who are unable to sleep if medication is taken late in the day should take the last dose before 6 p.m.

SR Tablets: Ritalin SR Tablets have a duration of action of approximately 8 hours. Therefore, Ritalin SR tablets may be used in place of Ritalin tablets when the 8 hour dosage of Ritalin SR corresponds to the titrated 8 hour dosage of Ritalin.

Children (6 years and over)

Ritalin should be initiated in small doses, with gradual weekly increments. Daily dosage above 60 mg is not recommended.

If improvement is not observed after appropriate dosage adjustment over a one-month period, the drug should be discontinued.

Tablets: Start with 5 mg twice daily (before breakfast and lunch) with gradual increments of 5 to 10 mg weekly.

SR Tablets: Ritalin SR tablets have a duration of action of approximately 8 hours. Therefore, Ritalin SR tablets may be used in place of Ritalin tablets when the 8 hour dosage of Ritalin SR corresponds to the titrated 8 hour dosage of Ritalin.

If paradoxical aggravation of symptoms or other adverse effects occur, reduce dosage or, if necessary, discontinue the drug.

Ritalin should be periodically discontinued to assess the child's condition. Improvement may be sustained when the drug is either temporarily or permanently discontinued.

italin® hydrochloride (methylphenidate hydrochloride USP)

Ritalin-SR® (methylphenidate hydrochloride)

Drug treatment should not and need not be indefinite and usually may be discontinued after puberty.

OVERDOSAGE

Signs and symptoms of acute overdosage, resulting principally from overstimulation of the central nervous system and from excessive sympathomimetic effects, may include the following: vomiting, agitation, tremors, hyperreflexia, muscle twitching, convulsions (may be followed by coma), euphoria, confusion, hallucinations, delirium, sweating, flushing, headache, hyperpyrexia, tachycardia, palpitations, cardiac arrhythmias, hypertension, mydriasis, and dryness of mucous membranes.

Treatment consists of appropriate supportive measures. The patient must be protected against self-injury and against external stimuli that would aggravate overstimulation already present. If signs and symptoms are not too severe and the patient is conscious, gastric contents may be evacuated by induction of emesis or gastric lavage. In the presence of severe intoxication, use a carefully titrated dosage of a *short-acting* barbiturate before performing gastric lavage.

Intensive care must be provided to maintain adequate circulation and respiratory exchange; external cooling procedures may be required for hyperpyrexia.

Efficacy of peritoneal dialysis or extracorporeal hemodialysis for Ritalin overdosage has not been established.

HOW SUPPLIED

Tablets 20 mg — round, pale yellow, scored (imprinted CIBA 34)
Bottles of 100 . . . . NDC 0083-0034-30
Bottles of 1000 . . . . NDC 0083-0034-40
Tablets 10 mg — round, pale green, scored (imprinted CIBA 3)
Bottles of 100 . . . . NDC 0083-0003-30
Bottles of 500 . . . . NDC 0083-0003-35
Bottles of 1000 . . . . NDC 0083-0003-40
Accu-Pak® Unit Dose (blister pack)
Box of 100 (strips of 10) . . . . NDC 0083-0003-32
Tablets 5 mg — round, yellow (imprinted CIBA 7)
Bottles of 100 . . . . NDC 0083-0007-30
Bottles of 500 . . . . NDC 0083-0007-35
Bottles of 1000 . . . . NDC 0083-0007-40
SR Tablets 20 mg — round, white, coated (imprinted CIBA 16)
Bottles of 100 . . . . NDC 0083-0016-30
Note: SR Tablets are color-additive free.

Do not store above 86°F (30°C). Protect from moisture.

Dispense in tight, light-resistant container (USP).

C82-63 (Rev. 1/83)

Serpasil®
reserpine USP   **Tablets**

DESCRIPTION

Reserpine, a pure crystalline alkaloid of rauwolfia, is a white or pale buff to slightly yellowish crystalline powder which darkens slowly on exposure to light and is insoluble in water. Chemically, is methyl-0-(3,4,5-trimethoxybenzoyl)-reserpate.

ACTIONS

Serpasil probably produces its antihypertensive effects through depletion of tissue stores of catecholamines (epinephrine and norepinephrine) from peripheral sites. This depression of sympathetic nerve function results in a decreased heart rate and a lowering of arterial blood pressure. In contrast, Serpasil's sedative and tranquilizing properties are thought to be related to depletion of 5-hydroxytryptamine from the brain.

Serpasil, like other rauwolfia compounds, is characterized by slow onset of action and sustained effects. Both cardiovascular and central nervous system effects may persist for a period of time following withdrawal of the drug.

INDICATIONS

Mild essential hypertension; also useful as adjunctive therapy with other antihypertensive agents in the more severe forms of hypertension; relief of symptoms in agitated psychotic states (eg, schizophrenia), primarily in those individuals unable to tolerate phenothiazine derivatives or those who also require antihypertensive medication.

CONTRAINDICATIONS

Known hypersensitivity, mental depression (especially with suicidal tendencies), active peptic ulcer, ulcerative colitis, and patients receiving electroconvulsive therapy.

WARNINGS

Extreme caution should be exercised in treating patients with a history of mental depression. Discontinue the drug at first sign of despondency, early morning insomnia, loss of appetite, impotence, or self-deprecation. Drug-induced depression may persist for several months after drug withdrawal and may be severe enough to result in suicide.

MAO inhibitors should be avoided or used with extreme caution.

Usage in Pregnancy

The safety of reserpine for use during pregnancy or lactation has not been established; therefore, the drug should be used in pregnant patients or in women of childbearing potential only when, in the judgment of the physician, it is essential to the welfare of the patient. Increased respiratory tract secretions, nasal congestion, cyanosis, and anorexia may occur in neonates and breast-fed infants of reserpine-treated mothers since reserpine crosses the placental barrier and also appears in maternal breast milk.

PRECAUTIONS

Since Serpasil increases gastrointestinal motility and secretion, it should be used cautiously in patients with a history of peptic ulcer, ulcerative colitis, or gallstones (biliary colic may be precipitated).

Caution should be exercised when treating hypertensive patients with renal insufficiency since they adjust poorly to lowered blood pressure levels.

Use Serpasil cautiously with digitalis and quinidine since cardiac arrhythmias have occurred with rauwolfia preparations.

Preoperative withdrawal of reserpine does not assure that circulatory instability will not occur. It is important that the anesthesiologist be aware of the patient's drug intake and consider this in the overall management, since hypotension has occurred in patients receiving rauwolfia preparations. Anticholinergic and/or adrenergic drugs (eg, metaraminol, norepinephrine) have been employed to treat adverse vagocirculatory effects.

ADVERSE REACTIONS

Rauwolfia preparations have caused gastrointestinal reactions including hypersecretion, nausea, vomiting, anorexia, and diarrhea; cardiovascular reactions including angina-like symptoms, arrhythmias (particularly when used concurrently with digitalis or quinidine), bradycardia; central nervous system reactions including drowsiness, depression, nervousness, paradoxical anxiety, nightmares, rare parkinsonian syndrome and other extrapyramidal tract symptoms, and CNS sensitization manifested by dull sensorium, deafness, glaucoma, uveitis, and optic atrophy. Nasal congestion is a frequent occurrence. Pruritus, rash, dryness of mouth, dizziness, headache, dyspnea, syncope, epistaxis, purpura and other hematologic reactions, impotence or decreased libido, dysuria, muscular aches, conjunctival injection, weight gain, breast engorgement, pseudolactation, and gynecomastia have been reported. These reactions are usually reversible and usually disappear after the drug is discontinued.

Water retention with edema in patients with hypertensive vascular disease may occur rarely, but the condition generally clears with cessation of therapy or with the administration of a diuretic agent.

DOSAGE AND ADMINISTRATION

For Hypertension: In the average patient not receiving other antihypertensive agents, the usual initial dose is 0.5 mg daily for 1 or 2 weeks. For maintenance, reduce to 0.1 mg to 0.25 mg daily. Higher doses should be used cautiously, because serious mental depression and other side effects may be increased considerably.

For Psychiatric Disorders: The usual initial dose is 0.5 mg, with a range of 0.1 mg to 1.0 mg. Adjust dosage upward or downward according to the patient's response.

Concomitant use of Serpasil with ganglionic blocking agents, guanethidine, veratrum, hydralazine, methyldopa, chlorthalidone, or thiazides necessitates careful titration of dosage with each agent.

Serpasil® (reserpine USP) Tablets

OVERDOSAGE

Signs and Symptoms

Impairment of consciousness may occur and may range from drowsiness to coma, depending upon the severity of overdosage. Flushing of the skin, conjunctival injection, and pupillary constriction are to be expected. Hypotension, hypothermia, central respiratory depression, and bradycardia may develop in cases of severe overdosage. Diarrhea may also occur.

Treatment

Evacuate stomach contents, taking adequate precautions against aspiration and for the protection of the airway; instill activated charcoal slurry.

Treat the effects of reserpine overdosage symptomatically. If hypotension is severe enough to require treatment with a vasopressor, use one having a direct action upon vascular smooth muscle (eg, phenylephrine, levarterenol, metaraminol). Since reserpine is long-acting, observe the patient carefully for at least 72 hours, administering treatment as required.

HOW SUPPLIED

Tablets, 0.1 mg — white (imprinted 35 CIBA)
   Bottles of 100 . . . . NDC 0083-0035-30
   Bottles of 1000 . . . . NDC 0083-0035-40

Tablets, 0.25 mg — white, scored (imprinted 36 CIBA)
   Bottles of 100 . . . . NDC 0083-0036-30
   Bottles of 500 . . . . NDC 0083-0036-35
   Bottles of 1000 . . . . NDC 0083-0036-40
   Bottles of 5000 . . . . NDC 0083-0036-45
   Consumer Pack — One Unit
      (12 bottles-100 tablets each) . . . . NDC 0083-0036-65

Dispense in tight, light-resistant container (USP).

C81-15   (5/81)

CIBA Pharmaceutical Company
Division of CIBA-GEIGY Corporation
Summit, New Jersey 07901

Geigy

Tofranil®
imipramine hydrochloride USP

Indications *Depression:* For the relief of symptoms of depression. Endogenous depression is more likely to be alleviated than other depressive states. One to three weeks of treatment may be needed before optimal therapeutic effects are evident.

Childhood Enuresis: May be useful as temporary adjunctive therapy in reducing enuresis in children aged 6 years and older, after possible organic causes have been excluded by appropriate tests. In patients having daytime symptoms of frequency and urgency, examination should include voiding cystourethrography and cystoscopy, as necessary. The effectiveness of treatment may decrease with continued drug administration.

Contraindications The concomitant use of monoamine oxidase inhibiting compounds is contraindicated. Hyperpyretic crises or severe convulsive seizures may occur in patients receiving such combinations. The potentiation of adverse effects can be serious, or even fatal. When it is desired to substitute Tofranil in patients receiving a monoamine oxidase inhibitor, as long an interval should elapse as the clinical situation will allow, with a minimum of 14 days. Initial dosage should be low and increases should be gradual and cautiously prescribed.

The drug is contraindicated during the acute recovery period after a myocardial infarction. Patients with a known hypersensitivity to this compound should not be given the drug. The possibility of cross-sensitivity to other dibenzazepine compounds should be kept in mind.

Warnings
Children: A dose of 2.5 mg/kg/day of imipramine hydrochloride should not be exceeded in childhood. ECG changes of unknown significance have been reported in pediatric patients with doses twice this amount.

Extreme caution should be used when this drug is given to:
   patients with cardiovascular disease because of the possibility of conduction defects, arrhythmias, congestive heart failure, myocardial infarction, strokes and tachycardia. These patients require cardiac surveillance at all dosage levels of the drug;

   patients with increased intraocular pressure, history of urinary retention, or history of narrow-angle glaucoma because of the drug's anticholinergic properties;

   hyperthyroid patients or those on thyroid medication because of the possibility of cardiovascular toxicity;

   patients with a history of seizure disorder because this drug has been shown to lower the seizure threshold;

   patients receiving guanethidine, clonidine, or similar agents, since imipramine hydrochloride may block the pharmacologic effects of these drugs;

   patients receiving methylphenidate hydrochloride. Since methylphenidate hydrochloride may inhibit the metabolism of imipramine hydrochloride, downward dosage adjustment of imipramine hydrochloride may be required when given concomitantly with methylphenidate hydrochloride.

Tofranil may enhance the CNS depressant effects of alcohol. Therefore, it should be borne in mind that the dangers inherent in a suicide attempt or accidental overdosage with the drug may be increased for the patient who uses excessive amounts of alcohol. (See **Precautions**.)

Since imipramine hydrochloride may impair the mental and/or physical abilities required for the performance of potentially hazardous tasks, such as operating an automobile or machinery, the patient should be cautioned accordingly.

Precautions
An ECG recording should be taken prior to the initiation of larger-than-usual doses of imipramine hydrochloride and at appropriate intervals thereafter until steady state is achieved. (Patients with any evidence of cardiovascular disease require cardiac surveillance at all dosage levels of the drug. See **Warnings**.) Elderly patients and patients with cardiac disease or a prior history of cardiac disease are at special risk of developing the cardiac abnormalities associated with the use of imipramine hydrochloride.

It should be kept in mind that the possibility of suicide in seriously depressed patients is inherent in the illness and may persist until significant remission occurs. Such patients should be carefully supervised during the early phase of treatment with imipramine hydrochloride, and may require hospitalization. Prescriptions should be written for the smallest amount feasible.

Hypomanic or manic episodes may occur, particularly in patients with cyclic disorders. Such reactions may necessitate discontinuation of the drug. If needed, imipramine hydrochloride may be resumed in lower dosage when these episodes are relieved. Administration of a tranquilizer may be useful in controlling such episodes.

An activation of the psychosis may occasionally be observed in schizophrenic patients and may require reduction of dosage and the addition of a phenothiazine.

Concurrent administration of imipramine hydrochloride and electroshock therapy may increase the hazards; such treatment should be limited to those patients for whom it is essential, since there is limited clinical experience.

Usage During Pregnancy and Lactation:
   Animal reproduction studies have yielded inconclusive results

Tofranil® imipramine hydrochloride USP

There have been no well-controlled studies conducted with pregnant women to determine the effect of imipramine hydrochloride on the fetus. However, there have been clinical reports of congenital malformations associated with the use of the drug. Although a causal relationship between these effects and the drug could not be established, the possibility of fetal risk from the maternal ingestion of imipramine hydrochloride cannot be excluded. Therefore, imipramine hydrochloride should be used in women who are or might become pregnant only if the clinical condition clearly justifies potential risk to the fetus.

Limited data suggest that imipramine hydrochloride is likely to be excreted in human breast milk. As a general rule, a woman taking a drug should not nurse since the possibility exists that the drug may be excreted in breast milk and be harmful to the child.

Usage in Children: The effectiveness of the drug in children for conditions other than nocturnal enuresis has not been established.

The safety and effectiveness of the drug as temporary adjunctive therapy for nocturnal enuresis in children less than 6 years of age has not been established.

The safety of the drug for long-term, chronic use as adjunctive therapy for nocturnal enuresis in children 6 years of age or older has not been established; consideration should be given to instituting a drug-free period following an adequate therapeutic trial with a favorable response.

A dose of 2.5 mg/kg/day should not be exceeded in childhood. ECG changes of unknown significance have been reported in pediatric patients with doses twice this amount.

Patients should be warned that imipramine hydrochloride may enhance the CNS depressant effects of alcohol. (See **Warnings**.)

Imipramine hydrochloride should be used with caution in patients with significantly impaired renal or hepatic function.

Patients who develop a fever and a sore throat during therapy with imipramine hydrochloride should have leukocyte and differential blood counts performed. Imipramine hydrochloride should be discontinued if there is evidence of pathological neutrophil depression.

Prior to elective surgery, imipramine hydrochloride should be discontinued for as long as the clinical situation will allow.

In occasional susceptible patients or in those receiving anticholinergic drugs (including antiparkinsonism agents) in addition, the atropine-like effects may become more pronounced (e.g., paralytic ileus). Close supervision and careful adjustment of dosage is required when imipramine hydrochloride is administered concomitantly with anticholinergic drugs.

Avoid the use of preparations, such as decongestants and local anesthetics, which contain any sympathomimetic amine (e.g., epinephrine, norepinephrine), since it has been reported that tricyclic antidepressants can potentiate the effects of catecholamines.

Caution should be exercised when imipramine hydrochloride is used with agents that lower blood pressure.

Imipramine hydrochloride may potentiate the effects of CNS depressant drugs.

Patients taking imipramine hydrochloride should avoid excessive exposure to sunlight since there have been reports of photosensitization.

Both elevation and lowering of blood sugar levels have been reported with imipramine hydrochloride use.

The Tofranil tablets (10, 25, 50 mg) contain FD&C Yellow No. 5 (tartrazine) which may cause allergic-type reactions (including bronchial asthma) in certain susceptible individuals. Although the overall incidence of FD&C Yellow No. 5 (tartrazine) sensitivity in the general population is low, it is frequently seen in patients who also have aspirin hypersensitivity.

Adverse Reactions Note: Although the listing which follows includes a few adverse reactions which have not been reported with this specific drug, the pharmacological similarities among the tricyclic antidepressant drugs require that each of the reactions be considered when imipramine is administered.

Cardiovascular: Orthostatic hypotension, hypertension, tachycardia, palpitation, myocardial infarction, arrhythmias, heart block, ECG changes, precipitation of congestive heart failure, stroke.

Psychiatric: Confusional states (especially in the elderly) with hallucinations, disorientation, delusions; anxiety, restlessness, agitation; insomnia and nightmares; hypomania; exacerbation of psychosis.

Neurological: Numbness, tingling, paresthesias of extremities; incoordination, ataxia, tremors; peripheral neuropathy; extrapyramidal symptoms; seizures, alterations in EEG patterns; tinnitus.

Anticholinergic: Dry mouth, and, rarely, associated sublingual adenitis; blurred vision, disturbances of accommodation, mydriasis; constipation, paralytic ileus; urinary retention, delayed micturition, dilation of the urinary tract.

Allergic: Skin rash, petechiae, urticaria, itching, photosensitization; edema (general or of face and tongue); drug fever; cross-sensitivity with desipramine.

Hematologic: Bone marrow depression including agranulocytosis; eosinophilia; purpura; thrombocytopenia.

Gastrointestinal: Nausea and vomiting, anorexia, epigastric distress, diarrhea; peculiar taste, stomatitis, abdominal cramps, black tongue.

Endocrine: Gynecomastia in the male; breast enlargement and galactorrhea in the female; increased or decreased libido, impotence; testicular swelling; elevation or depression of blood sugar levels.

Other: Jaundice (simulating obstructive); altered liver function; weight gain or loss; perspiration; flushing; urinary frequency; drowsiness, dizziness, weakness and fatigue; headache; parotid swelling; alopecia; proneness to falling.

Withdrawal Symptoms: Though not indicative of addiction, abrupt cessation of treatment after prolonged therapy may produce nausea, headache and malaise.

Note In enuretic children treated with Tofranil the most common adverse reactions have been nervousness, sleep disorders, tiredness, and mild gastrointestinal disturbances. These usually disappear during continued drug administration or when dosage is decreased. Other reactions which have been reported include constipation, convulsions, anxiety, emotional instability, syncope, and collapse. All of the adverse effects reported with adult use should be considered.

How Supplied Triangular, sugar-coated, coral-colored tablets of 10 mg in bottles of 100 and 1000; round, sugar-coated, coral-colored (black Geigy imprint) tablets of 25 mg in bottles of 100, 1000 and 5000 and unit strip packages of 100; round, sugar-coated, coral-colored (white Geigy imprint) tablets of 50 mg in bottles of 100, 1000 and 5000 and unit strip packages of 100; ampuls for intramuscular administration only, each containing 25 mg in 2 cc of solution (1.25%), in boxes of 10.

Note On storage, very minute crystals may form in some ampuls. This has no influence on the therapeutic efficacy of

Tofranil® imipramine hydrochloride USP

the preparation, and the crystals redissolve when the affected ampuls are immersed in hot tap water for one minute.

Dispense in tight container (USP).

C80-3   (1/80)

GEIGY Pharmaceuticals
Division of CIBA-GEIGY Corporation
Ardsley, New York 10502

*For complete details, please see
full prescribing information.*

(12/82) 117-3879